Readers Respond to *O My God*:

"Beautiful! Powerful! There are sooo many gems that touched my mind and heart—phenomenal insights ... incredibly valuable." ~ *JC, trauma survivor and free spirit*

"What a comforting book. What an incredible read. Beautifully described insights and intimate details of Celia, of others, of her relationship with God. I didn't actually want the conversation to end but I ended up finding a prayer in almost every line. So it really doesn't end." ~ *DA, trauma survivor and sober alcoholic*

"Brilliant ... Impeccable ... Fascinating ... Intoxicating ... Mind-bogglingly succinct ... Naturally elegant ... The truth-telling and humour is pure elixir. A book about spiritual and emotional healing; a beautiful and inviting treasure, a precious reveal of heart-centred truths and a quest for the good. Celia describes serious losses with care and unflinching clarity. There is great wisdom here for those who value truth and integrity and shudder at lies. Celia is startlingly sincere and devoted, *and* wild and untameable. Her reader will gladly trundle down any alley with her, or into any number of bars, knowing they are in her capable hands. *O My God* will be of great interest even to people who do not adhere to any religion or even spiritual tradition, to anyone wanting to feel less alone. Celia does a piece of our journey for us." ~ *AS, trauma survivor and life poet*

"I am in awe of Celia's courage in not only daring to be true to herself, but also in being willing to expose that self to others." ~ *Hennie, found in these pages*

By Celia McBride

THEATRE
So Many Doors

FILM
Last Stop for Miles

CELIA MCBRIDE

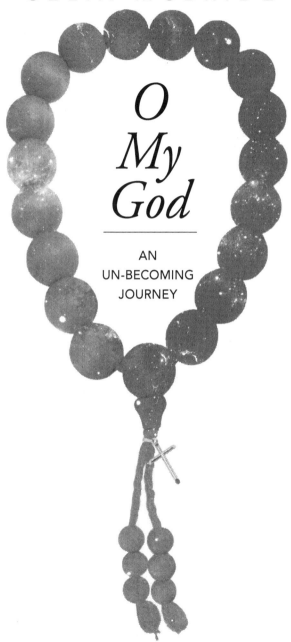

O
My
God

AN
UN-BECOMING
JOURNEY

INTOXICATING ... DARING ... UNFLINCHING ...

O My God
Copyright © 2022 by Celia McBride

Tellwell Talent
www.tellwell.ca

ISBN
978-0-2288-0536-6 (Paperback)
978-0-2288-0537-3 (eBook)

for the still suffering

"For me to be a saint means to be myself."
~ *Thomas Merton*

"God is the condition of possibility of any entity whatsoever, including ourselves. God is the answer to why there is something rather than nothing."
~ *Terry Eagleton*

JOURNEY POINTS

PART THREE
GIVING UP

PART FOUR
RISING UP

TO BE CLEAR ...

For a while, the working subtitle of this book was *A Journey of Un-Belief.* "Unbelief" was a play on the word "unbelievable" (because ending up in a convent, for me, was), and the term "unbeliever," which Christians often use to describe non-Christians. You see, technically I am an unbeliever. I don't actually *believe* in God, although at one time I would have said that I did. Belief is fickle, however, and it erodes over time. Today, I would say God is not someone I believe in. God is something I experience.

Throughout the book, when I refer to God, I am not talking about the Sky God, represented by antiquated depictions of a white man with a white beard directing human activity from the white clouds. That God, burdened by religious history and fanaticism, catastrophically divides the very children "He" is supposed to be looking after. Don't get me wrong, this Heavenly Man-God works well for a lot of people, but

God, if nothing else, is a shape-shifter. For me, God can be anything because God is Every Thing.

Science provides proof that everything seen and unseen is made of the same stuff, called Energy. By exchanging the word Energy for the word God, I am able to see that there is no thing that God is not, and that whatever God is, It is in no way separate from Who and What We Are.

I use many names to describe That Which Cannot Be Named or Described (and I capitalize those names, much to the chagrin of my editors), but the G-word prevails in these pages because, despite its divisiveness, it's a perfectly good word: simple, short, apt. It does the job. But, for God's sake, when I tell you I am praying to the Lord, please remember: It's Way Beyond That.

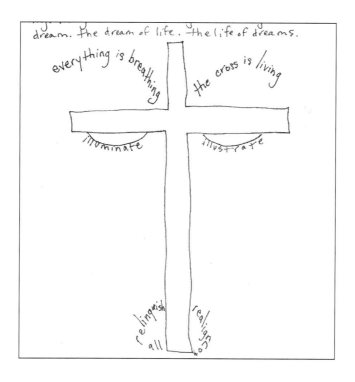

dream. the dream of life. the life of dreams.

everything is breathing   the cross is living

illuminate   illustrate

relinquish all   realign

PART ONE
GROWING UP

ARRIVAL

breathing
in us
living
in us
it is
all that
we are

When I was born I got my face bashed in.

"You came out face-first," my mother tells me.

Face-first? Who comes out face-first? A very small percentage of newborns, apparently. We are malpresentations of the facial variety and this kind of delivery is generally classified as birth trauma. Right from the get-go, I was f*cked.

A water-stained Kodak-colour photograph taken on the day I arrived home shows a tiny face covered in raw, red bruises. The sunny-yellow bunting bag wrapped around my little body cannot disguise the fact that I look like a boxer after a fight.

It was September 1971, in Whitehorse, Yukon Territory. Canada's Far North. "A gorgeous time of year," my mother wrote on a birthday card, decades later. "There was a glazing of ice on the puddles and the trees were electric yellow."

Was I fighting to get out because I couldn't wait to be born? Maybe. The persistence I showed in my birth-story certainly set up a life-long pattern of pushing myself too hard.

Gotta get there first. Gotta win!

Of needing to see and be seen.

Craning my neck forward to check things out …
look at me doing it!

Of desiring the full, divine and human experience.

> *O, to be in the world*
> *Spirit now flesh,*
> *Alive in earthly form!*

I am a perfectionist-addict, curious seeker and vainglorious show-off, lover of God. Only the last attribute saves me from the turmoil caused by the rest.

When I say I'm in love with God what I really mean is that I am in love with Existence. Not just existing, for that can sometimes be what I do not love, but *the Actuality of my Existence*. That is what I am truly in love with. God is the Great Mystery of our collective being and I love this Mystery with all of my heart. The best part about it? This Love can be experienced as reciprocal.

My first experience of Divine Union happened early, at the age of three or four years old, when I discovered that pressing my fists into the hollows of my closed eyes produced exploding fireworks of every colour, dancing and pulsing, changing and shifting, taking me into outer space. But this was inner space! At that age, I would not have been able to say "this is God" but I somehow knew these mysterious images of colourful rolling clouds and fiery bursts of stars existing inside of my body *were* God, and I would do this ritual until my eyeballs hurt.

How did I know about God? It was mostly innate. Neither of my parents came from a religious family. I am a common Canadian mix of Irish, Scottish, English and French (which basically means white and Christian), yet both my maternal and paternal grandparents had essentially become atheists, or perhaps humanists, rejecting the Church after being raised in their respective Christian homes. My mother's parents, known to me and my three sisters as Granny Jayne and Jack (he never liked "Grandpa"), both grew up in the Protestant tradition. Granny Jayne thought a *dash* of Christian education was a good idea and so my mother and her three sisters occasionally attended both United Church of Canada and Unitarian services.

My paternal grandfather, Russell McBride, had been raised Catholic, but it didn't stick. My father recalls his dad telling the story of how he and his boyhood friends would all run and hide when they saw the priest coming down the road. As a hard-working adult, Russell preferred to sleep in on Sundays. My grandmother, Phyllis, was Protestant and took her children (my dad and aunt Cheryl) to the United Church because church-going was just what people did in the 1950s. My dad was baptized and attended Sunday School, but there was no real commitment to the faith, and their church attendance dwindled as he got older.

By the time my parents had me and my three sisters (Jessica, Clara and Melissa), any thought of going to church had gone out the window and none of us were baptized or christened or whatever it was called.

Primary school introduced me to the Sky God or the God of *The Lord's Prayer*, *O Canada* and *God Save the Queen*. My mother, Eve, a writer and an artist, would often say she believed in a "Greater Power of the Universe," but she would rail against any dogmatic version of God. While insisting to this day that she is a

Christian ("Of course I believe in the teachings of Jesus, who wouldn't?"), she loves to denounce religion for "impinging on natural and benevolent human instincts and dictating individual freedom of choice."

My father, Terry, says things like, "If God created the world, then who the hell created God?" He is a nature-loving lawyer who insists that his desire to die on a Yukon mountaintop has nothing to do with spirituality. "They bury you in the ground and the worms eat you." (I loved this line enough to put it in one of my films, years later.) As for Christianity, he is totally baffled by the fact that Christians believe that it is possible to have a personal relationship with Jesus and, while he might finally admit to being agnostic, his contempt for organized religion is no secret.

Because there was no God to reject and no religious structure to rebel against, I had no church to quit. Left to my own devices and at complete liberty to discover for myself the Great Mystery Behind Existence, I became a seeker. Instead of denouncing God, I went looking.

Where does one with a religious disposition turn when she does not have religion at home? In my case, to someone else's church. When I was five, I asked my parents if I could go to Sunday School with a playmate. It is a testament to their open-mindedness that they let me go. Though the experience is non-existent in my own memory, the story is now famous in the family circle: "You came home and tried to convert the whole family," my parents say.

"What kind of church was it?" I ask my mother.

"Baptist, I think."

What happened to me at that church service? Where was this newfound holy desire coming from? Was I simply enthralled, as so many children are, by a nice-looking man named Jesus who *loved me* "for the Bible told me so"? Was I moved by the welcome from a church family, kindly people who embraced me and celebrated together with songs and stories? Or was my little heart, already on fire with adoration for the Cosmos-behind-my-eyes, newly touched by the charismatic energy of God, manifest in a long-ago story about Christ the Saviour?

Whatever it was, my fervour didn't last long. I did not continue attending church with my friend, and no one remembers why. But the seed of Christian curiosity, which took hold of me in later years, was probably planted in that primitive evangelical soil.

TRAUMA

remember
me.

love me.

honour me.

feel me.

During childhood, my spirituality was mainly being shaped by the experience of being brought up in the wilds of the Yukon. Our backyard was a vast wilderness, and I found great solace in the natural world. My older sister, Jessica, and I would spend hours running and playing with each other and our friends in the dense forest behind the house and on the steep and sometimes treacherous clay cliffs down the road. The land and the elements spoke to me, told me stories and taught me life lessons.

One of these lessons stands out: on a warm and sunny afternoon, I sat alone on a grassy incline not far from where we lived. The hill was covered with crocuses, and I remember being happy just sitting among them, watching the aspen leaves quiver and quake and wishing on the clouds floating above me. I remember picking a crocus and studying its pale, purple petals and bright, yellow centre. Upon this closer inspection, I noticed tiny, black bugs crawling up and down the soft, fuzzy stem. I gasped and dropped the flower. I may only have been five or six years old but the message was clear: beauty is not always what it seems. Look more closely and there are hidden realities to be found.

This lesson was driven home in a deeper way when, during a winter playdate with a friend, a broken branch jutting out from a cut log punctured a hole in my leg. I'd fallen off a woodpile and somehow the jagged protrusion had pushed its way through my snow pants, trousers and tights. As my mother removed each layer, trying to understand why I was screaming so loudly (because there was no blood), she finally discovered a perfect, quarter-sized hole on the inside of my little thigh. My tears stopped suddenly when I saw the mass of yellowish-white bumps where the skin had been broken.

"What's that?" I asked.

"I think those are your fat cells."

Fat cells? This peek at the mysterious physical world beneath my skin opened my mind to new questions. What were these bodies of ours? (My mother only heightened my fascination with the human body by telling us bedtime stories about the bugs that live on our eyebrows.)

These early experiences taught me to see that there was more to *everything* than meets the eye. Humans might be self-sufficient creatures driving cars and living in houses, but cut us open and we are fat and blood and muscle and bone. Look at our eyebrows under a microscope and discover bugs having a grand old time feeding on our dead skin cells. In my young mind, these phenomena, too, were God.

God was also given to me and Jessica via the Pioneer Girls, a Christian club for kids. I remember loving the experience. We got to wear a blue smock with a red sash, which we adorned with badges earned for completing special activities. We were introduced to scripture and its strange and archaic language. "Do unto others as you would have others do unto you." "Thy word is a lamp unto my feet, and a light unto my path." These passages drew me in and stayed with me into adulthood.

In 1979, we left the Yukon and moved to Toronto, Ontario. We went from a small town in the middle of nowhere to the big city in the centre of everything. I'd visited and stayed in big cities before but this was a radical change in all of our lives.

Like the proverbial one who just fell off the turnip truck, I was totally naïve. This hit home when I was laughed at by my classmates for bringing a giant zucchini from Granny Jayne and Jack's farm east of the city to school for Show and Tell. The kids' laughter taught me that it was not safe to be different, and the sense of rejection I felt began the painful journey of trying to fit in and belong.

I was a creative kid who loved sketching and acting and dancing and writing stories. I faithfully kept a diary starting at about the age of eight or nine. I was also athletic and found friendship and satisfaction in physical activities. My new school had a jogging program, and I was encouraged to join up for lunch-time runs to a nearby ravine. Mrs. Moon, the program's facilitator, was an odd duck (and she even looked a bit like the moon), but she was warm and friendly and made me feel welcome, odd-giant-zucchini-girl that I was.

In that first fall of our new life in Toronto, when I was turning eight, the weather was hot enough to feel like summer. The leaves on the trees were still fully green and the cicadas buzzed in the heat. The ravine that was our usual running route had thick bushes carpeting its steep sides, making it a secluded and lonely place, but we always jogged together, in groups or partners, and it never felt unsafe.

For some reason, on that particular September day, I and Jennifer, my jogging partner, had fallen behind the rest of the group. I think we were being lazy, not jogging at all, but walking and talking and goofing around. As we approached the foot of a bridge for cars that ran high overhead, we saw a man hanging around the bushes off to the side of the path. I remember feeling slightly nervous about seeing this lone stranger in "our" territory, but he ignored us, and we passed him by with no trouble.

We jogged to the first landmark where the group sometimes turned around, a boulder in the middle of the path. The others must have gone on to the next stopping-point that day, another marker further on. Jennifer and I decided we were tired and that we would go back to the school.

As we ran back along the path, we saw the same man still standing near the bottom of the bridge. This time he had his penis sticking out of his fly, and he was rubbing it with his finger. Jennifer and I clutched each other and giggled as we ran by. We didn't know what he was doing or what to think. We'd never seen any such thing in our lives. I remember turning back to look behind us. The man was now running toward us at full speed. No words can describe that feeling. We began to run.

Jennifer gained speed and was ahead of me. I remember the man grabbing me from behind. What I've never been quite sure of is whether he caught up to me or I stopped. And, if I did stop, why did I stop? My darkest thinking tells me I wanted to see what would happen. The shame from this idea has almost exceeded the shame generated by the incident itself. Whatever happened, I was now in his clutches and he leaned down over me, his face beside mine, my little body pulled against his. He shoved his hand down the elastic waist of my shorts and I felt his fingers fondle my privates. Then I felt warmth running down my legs. In terror, my bladder had let go and I'd peed on his hand.

He pulled his hand out and pushed me down, hard. I fell to the ground as he yelled, "Now, go!" I got up and ran. Jennifer was crying and she grabbed hold of me when I got to her. We ran up to the road to where a police car was parked at the top of the footpath. (It must have been there as a speed-trap for the cars that barrel down that section of city road.) Did we immediately tell those cops what had happened? No. Perhaps they could have caught that man if we had. But we acted as if everything was normal and ran past them. I remember thinking that we would get in trouble for doing something wrong.

We did tell the school and they called the police immediately. Sitting in the principal's office and trying to describe to the two male detectives what had happened was so embarrassing and so shameful, I could hardly speak. "Jerking off" was not in my vocabulary. All I could say was "his zipper was open" and let them figure out the rest.

The man was never caught. And I endured several difficult situations that arose from the incident, including having to identify a suspect, not in a protected room with two-way glass but in a bustling precinct full of men moving around, standing and sitting at desks. I chose the man who was staring at me even though I didn't really think it was him. I couldn't figure out why he was looking at me and I was terrified that I could be seen. We found out later I'd identified a plainclothes officer.

Life went on as normal and Mrs. Moon encouraged me to keep jogging. "If I have to tie a rope to my waist and yours so we can run together I'll gladly do it!" she said one day. But other than that, no one really acknowledged the experience. I remember re-living the terror one night in bed and, in distress, going downstairs to tell my mother. "Oh, sweetie," she said and hugged me. But I was given no follow-up counselling or support. PTSD was not a term anyone was familiar with. All the grown-ups just seemed to want to forget it, so I thought I'd better do the same. Years later, I asked my mother why everyone had acted like nothing happened. "That's what we were told to do," she said, "The school thought it would be the best thing for you if we played it down." *Played it down?* My young mind had been totally baffled. "Why is nobody freaking out about this?"

And where was God in all of this? One of the most common reasons people reject the idea of God is because of all of the suffering that takes place in the world. If there is a God why do these terrible things happen? How could any God allow a child to have her sexual innocence ripped away like that? It simply didn't occur to me to ask these questions and, within a year of the sexual trauma, at a sleepover with my new best friend, my faith proved to be unshakeable. As we lay in the quiet darkness falling toward sleep, I asked her if she believed in God.

"No," she answered immediately, confidently.

"I do," I whispered, with just as much confidence.

Wasn't I angry at God? Not then. Nowadays, I regularly partake in cathartic raging at God's seeming injustices, but as a girl, there was only this inexplicable, adoring love. My childhood faith baffles me. I don't know where I got it. I didn't give it to myself. For the most part, I kept it a secret. Secret prayers in bed, secret knowing.

Over the next number of years, my love of God was further fed and nurtured by summers spent at Camp Tapawingo, a YWCA camp in northern Ontario. Though Christian, Tapawingo was not evangelical. The camp's grounds did have giant crosses, one welcoming campers upon their arrival, and one marking the outdoor chapel atop a rocky outcrop overlooking Georgian Bay, where we would hike for the Sunday service in our best whites, but no one was preaching the Gospel. The land and its Indigenous peoples were acknowledged and honoured. We gave thanks to the Lord before meals and said evening prayers, but I don't remember directly connecting this to Jesus. I just loved singing *Johnny Appleseed* and *Taps* each day and night.

The YWCA's mild form of Christianity was appealing and valuable. It taught us kindness, generosity, teamwork, joy, service and how to love and appreciate nature. There was no mention of being saved, and yet the experience of being together with other girls and young women in that harmonizing environment did save us. We were accepted as we were, with or without a belief system.

I was fifteen years old the last summer I attended Tapawingo, and by that time I had discovered alcohol and drugs. On the inside, I still loved to sing songs to the Lord. On the outside, I had become too-cool-for-school. That meant getting wasted. I brought two joints to camp and bragged about it to one of the counsellors-in-training on the first day. She was kind enough to wait until the second-last day to report me.

"You have one minute to go and get the weed," the camp director said, after calling me into her cabin for what I thought would be a meeting to tell me how wonderful I was. When I held out the one joint upon my return (I'd already smoked the first one with a fellow camper), she looked at it as though it were the most harmless thing in the world. She had to follow protocol and I was told to phone my parents and tell them I was coming home.

"Hi, sweetie, what's up?" asked my father, obviously surprised to hear from me.

"I brought weed to camp and they're sending me home." Dead silence. Though it may have been the first time I disappointed my parents, it would not be the last, as the long road of active addiction and self-destructive behaviours began.

IN SEARCH OF ...

As a child, I could be sullen and wildly temperamental. Now, as a growing teenager who was drinking and using drugs, these charming qualities received an upgrade. Perhaps every teenager experiences ever-increasing mood swings and extreme desolation. Perhaps it wasn't the drugs but the trauma. I don't know. But I spent a lot of time feeling unhinged and inconsolable. Getting loaded with the cool kids brought relief and good times. The change was extreme. I went from being a straight-laced, choir-singing, nerdy kid with good marks to a lying, stealing, sexually-active adolescent who was failing in school. A diary entry from 1984, when I was just thirteen, two years prior to getting kicked out of camp, illustrates the beginnings of self-rejection and the longing to fit in:

> *Hi Di, Haven't written for ages. I just read this diary. God was I a wimp! Boy do I wanna be wasted right now. Can you see I've changed? See ya Dude.*

Teachers sat me down with my parents, who were distraught that all of their attempts to teach me right from wrong were being rebuffed. They were bewildered that I seemed hell-bent on self-destructing. Sense was talked into me. "This is not who you are," they all told me. I would cry, knowing they were right. But it didn't stop me. I quit the choir and stuck with the rebels.

Social workers came next. I found it difficult to talk to them. One was a man, and his office was a doctor's examination room in a hospital. Sitting too close to him for my comfort and staring at the cupboard labelled "gynecological instruments" totally shut me down. Another counsellor named Susan had more success, and I was able to share some of what was going on. Her kindness touched me. Years later, I ran into Susan on the street and told her I was thriving. It made her day, she said, and mine.

Still, Susan's overall impact was minimal, and I continued to gain a kind of sick satisfaction from being bad. I was drawn to the dark side, and partying fed my curious, restless spirit. No one forced me to get high. Peer pressure was more like peer attraction. Feeling inadequate, not liking myself, thinking I could be like "them" if I tried hard enough, motivated my actions. Being cool would make me acceptable, make me enough. If only someone had told me that the real definition of cool was to be myself! But self-acceptance wasn't taught in school and it wasn't really modelled at home. My parents both came from you're-never-good-enough families, and though they loved me and my sisters and taught us how to be good, productive people, they also criticized and emphasized our imperfections, unwittingly passing on patterns of low self-esteem.

Insecurity, mood swings, obsessive thinking and depressive energy made life challenging. One of my coping mechanisms was lying in bed and fantasizing about being a movie star or being in a relationship with a movie star. As I see it now, these fantasies were a kind of prayer: private communion with a remote and yet intimate power. They were also a way of self-regulating the ongoing mental torment over which I felt totally powerless:

> *Why do I always worry? Why won't this annoying, pessimistic fuck-shit voice in my head shut-up? It's not me — it bugs me constantly. I want to rid myself of it or at least be able to have more control of it — It makes me unhappy all the time. Shut-up — Shut-up for fucking once — OK — can't you!?! Won't you?! Sometimes I truly believe I know who I am. Other times I'm not so sure. The devil mother-fucker side takes over. Well, Fuck you! I am very very <= What means very? — (Drunk)*

Three months after getting kicked out of camp and two months into Grade 10, I got asked to leave the high school I was (barely) attending. As fate would have it, I got accepted into Etobicoke School of the Arts on the same day. One of my best friends had transferred to ESA, and I'd auditioned for the theatre program just a week prior so I could stay close to her. My acting had apparently been good enough to win me a spot. When I was a kid, I'd told my mother I wanted to be an actress when I grew up and she'd said, "Your whole life is an act." I took it as a compliment. ESA probably saved my life from going down the toilet. While I continued to party, I also put my heart and soul into becoming a good actress and a good student.

Theatre was good medicine. So were hallucinogenic drugs. I'm not kidding. Alcohol made me physically ill (not that it stopped me from drinking), and weed often made me paranoid (not that that stopped me from smoking it), but LSD, magic mushrooms and peyote expanded my mind and elevated my consciousness. Psychedelics made me want to be a better person and participate in the wonder of life. In the simplest of terms, they brought me closer to God.

Once, I had a long, strange acid trip with my own reflection in a bathroom mirror. While washing my hands, I caught my own eyes looking at me. Looking back, I smiled. The person in the mirror smiled back. Embarrassed, I laughed. She laughed, too. I looked away, looked back. She was still there, seeing me, smiling at me, enjoying this experience of being recognized.

This sensation of seeing *Celia*, witnessing myself outside of myself, distinct from my own movements and yet identical and completely in sync with my own, awakened me to the fact that my physical body was *animated*. And not by me.

Peyote, the mind-altering cactus plant used for spiritual purposes in some Indigenous cultures, brought me beautifully, momentously, into what I can only describe as Pure Love. I was Love. You were Love. Everything was Love. It was the most natural feeling in the world. Never had I been more comfortable in my own skin, more grounded in my own body. There was simply no separation between me and All That Existed. Pure Love and Pure Joy.

The creative focus through school and an elevated consciousness led me to seek further help for my despair. During the previous year, when things had gotten really bad, my mother had asked me if I wanted to see her therapist. I'd flatly refused. But something had changed and I wanted to get better. "I'm ready to accept help," I told my mum, and began seeing Anne, a psychotherapist.

"The first thing I should tell you is that I was sexually molested when I turned eight and I think that's why I'm so screwed up," I told Anne in our first session. We must have spent some time on this, but the only memory I have is of her simply saying, "Thank you for telling me that." Again, no treatment for trauma was offered.

Three other things stand out: The first is that Anne called me "Celie" and even had "Celie" written on my file, which sat at her feet during our sessions. My family thought this was hilarious, and the joke stuck because I'm still called Celie to this day by certain friends and family.

Secondly, our sessions brought healing to my relationship with my father. He and I had become somewhat estranged post-puberty because, as I'd begun to develop physically, I realized that my father was a *man* and consciously pulled back from him. His distancing may have been connected to my physical changes or they may have been due to his disappointment in my reckless behaviour. Regardless, we'd grown apart and it bothered me. At Anne's urging, I invited him to a session and tried to tell him all the things I couldn't say at home.

"So what you're really trying to say is …" Anne said, encouraging me to go on. Geez, was she actually going to make me say it *out loud*?

"That … I love you," I said, looking my father in the eye, choking on the words.

"I love you, too," he said, his own tears forming.

The third thing was that Anne encouraged me to nurture the part of me that loved nature and thrived in the wilderness. With her help, I applied and was accepted into a summer session at the Canadian Outward Bound Wilderness School.

In early August 1988, a month before turning 17 and after spending the first part of the summer getting fit by going to the gym and cycling 35km a day, I boarded a plane for Thunder Bay, Ontario, to take part in a 21-day outdoor adventure. As the plane took to the sky, I saw a rabbit hopping on the stretch of green grass between the runways. Like a wink from the Universe, I somehow knew it was there just for me.

Our group was a mix of privileged and at-risk youth. We were all given journals and encouraged to write about our experiences daily.

> *It didn't rain. A gift from God. Who am I now and who will I be in 21 days? I am not as unsure as I used to be but I still don't have answers to questions that constantly wrack my brain. Where will I go? What will I do? What will become of me. I want to do so much. How much of it is possible. There really is so little time. Shit, I'm nervous, excited and ready for anything. God help me be tolerant.*

The God of Creation, God of the Natural World, the Great Giver of rivers and forests and streams and mud bogs and beavers and big sky and rough waters was so close, so very close to me during that time. God was constantly making Itself known to me, waving at me, like the rabbit on the runway. Here, I belonged.

While on solo expedition, when I spent three days alone on the flat-rock shores of Sturgeon Lake, I entered into a great interior silence, maybe for the first time in my life. My home was a rudimentary shelter that I'd built in a smooth dip of rock a safe distance from the water. During the day, I would explore the neighbouring forest, dense with trees and carpeted with thick, spongy moss that glowed emerald green when the sun shone. At night, I slept out in the open, using a rock for a pillow, listening to the lake and contemplating the stars. On one of the nights, a strong wind woke me and I clutched my sleeping bag as I made my way back to the shelter, laughing out loud as it flew up above me like some puffy, upright flag. My journal records my wakened state:

> *I am constantly living in the future. Why not live for what is happening now?*

After three days of solitude the trip leaders picked us all up one-by-one in the canoes. We had been given an instruction to remain in the silence until we had all been collected and returned to our main camp. As we paddled together without speaking, held together by natural joy, an overwhelming desire to giggle consumed us.

> *I am loved. I can love back. Remember to give all you can. It's incredible how if you keep a positive attitude, everything seems to go well. Nothing can really go wrong. Things can go wrong but nothing is that big of a deal. Enjoy life. I love life, and I'm going to enjoy it. It's a nice attitude to have. If only I could see things that way all the time.*

But I couldn't. When I returned to Toronto to complete my last year of high school, I tried my hardest to stay clean, fit, healthy and focused on my well-being. I struggled.

> *I can't breathe. I hate the city and what the people do to the earth. It is getting harder and harder to stay happy. So many things make me sad.*

I had no practices, no teacher or guide to help me understand how to channel the euphoric states into practical living, something I would learn much later in life. Any spiritual equilibrium I did have was rocked by the partying, which I didn't seem able to give up.

After high school, I made my way back to the Yukon where all my intentions of being a nature-girl went out the window. In the dark of a Whitehorse winter, I found the bars and got sucked further into my partying ways.

On one of these wild nights, I met a man in a bar named Jim, a hippie from "Down South" who approached me on the dance floor where I was shaking my booty with a crowd of sweaty drunks. Jim was extremely tall and skinny, he had a full, bushy beard, wore a bandanna tied around his head and was dressed in filthy, ragged, unstylish clothes. But he paid attention to me and that won him the privilege of driving me home.

Sitting parked in his rusty, blue and white truck, sagging with the weight of a camper trimmed with grubby curtains, Jim leaned over and kissed me. At age eighteen, I had let many boys and men that I didn't know (or particularly like) kiss me and have their way with me (I'd lost my virginity on the cusp of fifteen) but Jim seemed keen to get to know me. He asked if he could take me to lunch the next day and even picked me up at the Whitehorse Star where I'd managed to get a job in the Circulation Department stuffing papers and counting coins.

After a trip to the salad bar, we settled into a booth and Jim leaned forward, his bright blue eyes shining, and said, "I believe in the Lord Jesus Christ who is our true Lord and only Saviour. How about you?"

I nearly choked on my radish. This sweet, good-looking fella was a Jesus freak! I got nervous. Maybe he was going to make me join a cult. I was intolerant of Jesus freaks. During high school, my friends and I would encounter them in bars and on the streets and make fun of what we perceived to be their total lack of self-awareness.

"No, that's not really my thing," I stuttered, avoiding Jim's piercing gaze, trying to be calm. When he walked me back to work he asked if he could see me again and

I said, "No," rudely, and left him at the door. Months later I saw his truck and camper sinking into the banks of the Yukon River, the dirty curtains still clinging to the windows.

Thinking back, I am struck by how afraid I was of his question. Granted I was eighteen years old, but wasn't I secretly curious about Jesus? Hadn't I loved Jesus at one time? Here was an opportunity to maybe ask a few questions, perhaps even dismantle my prejudice, which had grown out of my youthful fear of being different and my judgmental perception of anything that wasn't cool, but Jim's flashing blue eyes and reference to Jesus as Saviour immediately made him a psychopath in my eyes.

At the end of the non-stop party that was the summer of '90, and a love affair with Bill, a man 21 years my senior, I left Whitehorse for Montreal to begin my first year of university. I went from being a bar chick hanging with the bikers to being a freshman, living at home with my parents (who had moved to Montreal the year before for my father's work). The drinking and using had gotten out of control and my spiritual tank was pretty empty but I somehow managed to get my act together and just kept on trying to be okay.

> *my very soul ...*
> *an open wound ...*
> *hidden to everyone and everything ...*

During the next couple of years, while I studied English at Concordia and continued to try to find a balanced lifestyle, my sister Jessica started seeing a man named Richard, an agnostic who had been raised in an evangelical Christian family. Richard's roommate, Lucas, was studying for his Masters in Divinity, and talked about becoming a minister. The four of us would party together and hang out, engaging in intense philosophical and religious discussions.

Richard and Lucas introduced me to a liberal, progressive Christianity I had no idea existed. Here were two young men who were religious *and* cool. There was nothing freakish about these guys. They were often critical of Christianity's shortcomings and outspoken in their rejection of fundamentalist religiosity and blind faith, yet they talked about God without shame and saw beyond the literal interpretation of scripture. The Bible wasn't factual, they told me, but metaphorical and allegorical. Their passion for Jesus and his teachings, for what they considered to be his true message (service, inclusivity, love and justice), was very attractive.

Lucas and Richard attended a Presbyterian church in the West Island of Montreal where the minister was their good friend. Jessica and I went with them a couple of times and I was astonished to meet more people like them: smart, discerning and faithful. It was liberating to talk about God without fear of being judged.

Lucas also helped me to unpack my fear of the punishing Sky God, the God of Judeo-Christian culture. Curious life experiences had often made me feel like God was out to get me. Like the time a truck full of yahoos leaned out of their vehicle to yell obscenities at me. Or the numerous times I'd be walking along the sidewalk feeling confident and then suddenly twist my ankle. I was flummoxed by events like these. Why, when I felt good, would something bad happen? Was this God trying to teach me something or the Devil playing a trick?

"What if it's all God?" Lucas suggested.

His question invited me to start seeing that any situation could be changed by a shift in my perception. What if the Universe was not against me but for me? What if God was an Energy working in my favour every single moment of the day, calling me to become more conscious? Instead of seeing these levelling encounters as a punishment from some vengeful force or trickster Sky God, I could view them as a unifying wake-up call, an opportunity to come alive to my Highest Self.

I began to move from being secretly afraid of a patriarchal Devil/God who hammered me into submission through intimidation and shame to now *experiencing* Life as a benevolent, unifying teacher. This shift served me well. As the drug-and-alcohol addiction continued to progress and the dual existence of being a hardcore party-girl and a decent student went on, the notion that God was with me and for me fed my desire to do well in my English courses. I loved to write and received good marks in the classes I cared about. Multiple professors praised my essays and encouraged my skills.

> *I remain two separate people in one confused mind.*

Yup, I still loved to drink and get high. One night, alone in the apartment I shared with Jessica, I consumed an entire bottle of cheap white wine and smoked a big joint. This produced a terrifying paranoia. The world outside became an unsafe, hostile environment and my own mind felt like it was actively trying to kill me. With nowhere to run and panic mounting, something in me, my deepest knowing, told me I had no choice but to go straight into the fear. The only way to overcome it was to experience it, sit right inside of the mental chokehold. *Feel it.*

I closed my eyes and breathed deeply into the fright that gripped all my senses. No resistance. My thoughts began to speed up, shooting forward at warp speed, blasting through time and space in a tunnel of flashing colours and bright light, faster and faster and faster until wham! Everything stopped. A face appeared. I opened my eyes, shocked. It was the face of Jesus.

Instantly, the fear was gone. An intense peace had come over me. Then I got nervous. Did this mean I was supposed to go out and preach the Good News? Forget that. But after diving into the heart of fear, Jesus had shown up and saved me.

The importance of this event can be seen sprinkled throughout my writing in hidden and not-so-hidden Jesus references, first in poems and journal entries and then in the plays I began writing while attending the National Theatre School of Canada. Characters like Voula, an innocent Born-Again who murders her husband, began to express themselves on my behalf: "Jesus? I am a hellbound sinner," Voula says.

During my two years in the Playwriting Program at the NTSC, I found my voice as a writer. I also spent ridiculous amounts of time getting thoroughly blotto and untold hours of mental energy fantasizing and obsessing about an on-again-off-again sexual relationship with Jimmy, an acting student. But I managed to work hard and write prolifically, nearly ten plays in two years, and in 1995, upon graduating, I received a $10,000 Fox Fellowship to travel to Ireland to work with two different theatre companies.

Just before I left for Dublin, I went through a wormhole. Strutting along a Montreal street on a warm, sunny afternoon and feeling pretty sexy in some strappy heels, my foot hit an uneven section of sidewalk, bending my ankle and collapsing me to the ground in searing pain. Embarrassed, crying quietly and doing my best to act cool, I staggered to my feet and limped on with determined dignity. As I went to cross the road, black spots clouded my vision and the world around me suddenly disappeared.

> *A princess in an ancient land. My home a castle. Riding horses over green hills, married to a man who does the same. Battles and dragons and fire. One hundred years go by in real time.*

A circle of faces peering down at me, asking if I was okay, awakened me to the fact that I was in the middle of the street, cars only feet away, horns honking at me to move. Kind people helped me to the curb. How long had I been out? "Ten seconds." *Ten seconds?* But I'd just lived a hundred years in real time!

The following week, when I arrived in Dublin and walked out of the airport and into the damp, sea-filled air, the energy of the land came up through my feet and I felt, tangibly, actually, *in my blood*, that I had just returned home.

While working in Limerick with a theatre company doing a production of *Hamlet* in an 12th Century cathedral, I started seeing one of the actors. He was sweet and we had a nice relationship, though most of our sex and love was fuelled by copious amounts of the delicious black-and-white magic that is Guinness. One night during sex, the condom broke. I was pretty certain I was ovulating and we talked about what to do, deciding the morning-after pill was the best solution. Forty quid later I had a prescription and swallowed the two little pills on a busy street corner. There, on that grey, wet day in the middle of Limerick, I burst into spontaneous, shameful tears.

I cannot forgive myself.

For what? For the horrific thought that I was killing a potential future child by taking emergency contraception. Deeper still, for "allowing" the childhood sexual assault to happen because I'd (maybe) stopped in my tracks, and for the untold incidents of acting out in sexually inappropriate ways that had followed the trauma. In other words, for what amounted to a pretty big cauldron of shame.

I remember pulling myself together and crossing the street in the rain. Despite the seeming hopelessness of the revelation, it was actually a relief to be given this insight. It explained a lot. No wonder I was miserable, I blamed myself for being human!

After the three-month fellowship, I decided to let the return airline ticket go and found a shared flat in Dublin. I'd fallen in love with the land and the people and I was having the time of my life with all my drinking friends. I continued to write and had some success, winning a place in a national theatre competition and receiving a promise from a theatre company to produce *Choke My Heart*, my play about two giant artichokes that grow from the soil of a family's hidden sexual secrets.

After fifteen months, I was ready to go back to Canada. Arriving in Ireland had felt like returning to my ancestral home but it was definitely time for me to go home-home.

BOTTOMING OUT

THE CROSS

HAS NO

BOUNDS

IT STRETCHES

INFINITELY

IN ALL

DIRECTIONS.

T hree months after arriving back in Montreal, I promptly left for Edmonton, Alberta, to start a theatre company with Jimmy, the on-again-off-again obsession from the National Theatre School. The wise part of me knew I was likely walking back into a toxic jumble of drunken sex and mind games, but we'd agreed to just be friends, so I borrowed money from my parents to take a train across the country to try it out.

Things fell apart within a very short time. Jimmy and I rented an apartment together and the drunken sex resumed. This time, something in me resisted the toxic pattern, and he quickly found another woman to stay with, leaving me with a six-month lease on an apartment with no furniture. Asking my parents for more money to get back to Montreal was simply not an option. Sticking around and saving up to buy a plane ticket was the only foreseeable way out.

I found a waitressing job in a brand-new Chinese restaurant within walking distance from the apartment. It was owned by a Chinese couple from Hong Kong, who had left when the Crown colony was handed over to China. Because I was white, they believed I was their lucky charm, and because of their generosity and kindness, I believed they were mine. This couple treated me like royalty, feeding me not once but twice during my six-hour shift and inviting me into their personal lives, taking me out for Dim Sum and bringing me to their suburban house on the outskirts of the city for a family celebration.

At that time, 1997, $5.00 an hour was the going rate for a waitress. I was working a 30-hour week and taking home $150. Tips were scant. There were very few customers and if I managed to make more than $20 in a week I felt like I'd hit the jackpot. If I was going to save enough money to leave my hellish living situation I would have to do something drastic: stay out of the bars and stop buying dope.

This saving-money strategy had an unexpected bonus: for the first time in years there was no alcohol and no drugs in my system. Just like with my health-stint during the summer of Outward Bound, I started to come alive, even splurging on a cheap pair of running shoes so I could jog around the track in a nearby schoolyard on my days off.

One day, as I walked to work on a sunny but cold March afternoon with this newfound sober energy coursing through my body, I felt the words *I am an alcoholic* rise up inside of me. The energetic sensation in my body reminded me of being a little kid again, running along the street, happy, joyous and free. I was liberated from all toxins, unburdened, untouched, alive.

Then I discovered a book called *The Universe and Beyond* by Terence Dickenson. Out of boredom one night at the restaurant I decided to clean the dusty shelves below the cash register. Underneath elastics and paper clips, the book appeared as though by magic, warped and puffy from water stains. Its cover photograph of cosmic gases exploding in a kaleidoscope of colours recalled my childhood God-behind-my-eyes. Each evening, I would pore over its pages, marvelling at the pictures and descriptions of white dwarves and black holes and trying to grasp the numbers. The Milky

Way's diameter is somewhere around 120,000 light years across? There are one hundred billion galaxies? One light year measures 9 trillion kilometres?

Synchronistically, the comet Hale-Bopp appeared in the sky. Night after night, I'd come home from the restaurant and stand in the back yard to watch the bright space-tadpole with the 50 million km-long tail streaking across the stars. The newspaper reported the comet to be moving at about 156,000 km/hr, but from one evening to the next it remained in the same spot!

How small was I? How small were my problems relative to these numbers and these galactic bodies? The Universe was sharply putting my little life into perspective, both reinforcing my insignificance and reminding me that I was a part of it all. The notion that I was unforgivable became less believable. On a tiny piece of paper, I wrote out an apology for my transgressions, folded it into the smallest square possible and placed it in the pocket of my work trousers, its energy providing a daily reminder to be humble.

Cosmic Energy was my lifeline during those four months in Edmonton. The fear that Jimmy would come back to the apartment and we would have a confrontation was ever-present, the upstairs neighbours were often drunk and loud, and the loneliness was sometimes unbearable. I was now praying regularly and fervently to this God of Synchronicity and it was carrying me through.

Spring was showing its face and the money in the bank was increasing. At the end of March, about halfway to my goal of leaving Edmonton, I was drawn to attend the Easter Sunday service at a Ukrainian Catholic Church. I'd passed the building each day on my way to the restaurant and something drew me into the cavernous church on that sunny but still-cold-for-spring morning. I didn't know anything about Catholicism or what I was getting into but I felt consoled by the colourful icons of Jesus and the saints painted on the walls and ceilings. The congregation numbered in the hundreds, the entire service was in Ukrainian and I was wedged into a pew between families who totally ignored me, but that did not stop the tears and mucus from streaming down my face during the liturgy.

The truth Love breathes into us.

What truth? I didn't have any concept of Christ being "The Truth and the Light" as Christianity professes Jesus to be. But something had cracked me open. I'd been reading the book *Dead Man Walking* by Sister Helen Prejean, and her selflessness, her sense of mercy, and her ability to forgive, accept, and unconditionally love incarcerated men living on death row, made me even more curious about Jesus, who was her example and her beloved teacher. I really wanted what she had.

> *I can see myself*
> *a nun*
> *who once was a*
> *playwright.*

Finally the day came when I could afford to leave Edmonton. It was May 1997. I'd spent four months in a freezing apartment and the air outside had finally turned warm. It was hard to leave the family who had hired me. We'd become friends. But there was no question I had to go. I'd been staying sober on my own but on a trip to see friends and family in BC, I found myself drunk on a number of occasions, unable to say no to the drink.

Back in Montreal, moving in with my parents felt like an epic fail. I was about to start work as a nanny (again), and even though I adored the two kids with all of my heart, I was not happy about sitting on my unproduced plays, waiting, and wondering what to do next. I'd decided that since I couldn't abstain from booze and dope entirely I would simply just have to control it. Moderate my intake. Balance the amounts. Journal entries show despair:

> *I'm drinking.*
> *I'm drinking again.*
> *What can I tell you?*
> *Trying not to punish myself*
> *knowing I'd rather be sober*
> *aware of how I can't.*

And faith:

> *God is present. You've got the guide of your god.*

In the spring of '98, I directed *Hitching a Ride*, one of my plays, for a spring theatre festival. I cast Liam, an actor I'd known casually as a friend, in one of the parts, and by the end of the production we'd fallen madly in love. On one of our first dates, I told him I was an alcoholic. We were in a bar and I was drinking a pitcher of beer but I was serious! He told me his mother was a recovering alcoholic and a part of me longed to be able to say those words about myself.

Our timing to start a relationship wasn't great because I was heading back to Ireland for the premiere of *Choke My Heart* and had a vague plan to move there permanently. We tried to convince ourselves that we'd merely had a torrid love affair and saying good-bye was simply part of its bittersweet nature.

When I landed in Dublin I headed straight to the pub to meet my old friends. I remember having one pint of Guinness and telling myself that was all. Someone put another pint in front of me and it sat there for over an hour. Then I drank it. Then I drank another one. And another one. I don't know how many I had but the next morning I woke up late, barely able to move. I couldn't stand up straight in the shower and my body was sick at both ends. When I rang for a taxi to take me to the train station it took an hour to arrive and I remember throwing up in the bushes of my friend's garden while I waited.

Dublin is not a big city and it's certainly not big enough to accommodate all of the cars that want to get into its centre. I had forgotten this little fact and the traffic was so bad it took another hour to get to the station. Of course, I missed my train and the first day of rehearsal. I had to ring the theatre company and tell them that I, the guest of honour, wouldn't be there. The next train was five hours later. Since I'd packed for a permanent move, including all the paper copies of my plays, I had two suitcases weighing a thousand pounds each and I arranged them like a fortress around a bench in the station where I passed out, waking with a start every once in a while to check the time.

The director of the play picked me up and I fumbled for an excuse. He made a joke about the weight of my luggage and, embarrassed, I said nothing about my plan to stay in the country forever. The next day, I apologized profusely to the company, but they laughed it off, figuring I'd gone overboard on my first night back.

The company had high hopes for the play. "I think we're all going to be stars," said one of the actors. After the thrill of opening night, blind drunk, I lay in bed in the rented flat I'd been given as part of my contract, and wept. "I have everything I want," I sobbed. "I have everything I want." True love and career success and it still wasn't enough.

The play, with its f-bombs and incestuous characters, got a couple of decent reviews and a couple of scathing reviews. Word got out about the incest and people stayed away in droves. The company had expected we would tour the country and beyond but, much to everyone's disappointment, we closed with no hope of going any further. I returned to Montreal and moved in with Liam and his two roommates. Liam's bedroom became our sanctuary of love and closeness but my mind wasn't right. I was now telling myself to stay away from booze and this effort produced a mental obsession: to drink or not to drink. This brain battle caused terrible emotional and spiritual suffering. Perhaps only an addict can understand that kind of torture.

In my desperation, I began to think that God was calling me to have a child. I liken this now to a drowning person grabbing for a life preserver, anything to deliver me from my hopelessness. Having a child would save me. And save the world, too. I had enough awareness to know that fantasies had long been my way of escaping the discomfort of reality but this particular fantasy felt real enough to be believed.

> *I would like to have my baby soon. A prophecy to fulfil.*

It wasn't too difficult to convince Liam. He'd already asked me to marry him and I'd said yes with the stipulation that we keep it a secret—perhaps I had a sense of what was to come.

Before long my breasts began to feel sore and I knew I was pregnant. On fire with happiness, I went to see my family doctor and she confirmed that I was five weeks, congratulating me and giving me a stash of folic acid samples to help prevent birth defects. On the bus ride home, I had a vision of myself in nine months time, sporting a huge belly, and shame rose to my cheeks. Then, despair.

> *I cannot be reassured*
> *how I try*
> *to recall*
> *the faith I had*
> *I pray*
> *and lose track of my god*

Seven weeks into the pregnancy, I felt some cramping and wetness between my legs. When I reached down with my fingers to investigate they came back covered in blood. I had remembered that spotting in early pregnancy was normal but the cramps intensified. Sitting on the toilet, the blood gushed forth and I heard a *plop*. A mass of tissue and blood floated in the toilet bowl. Seconds after I flushed it I froze, mortified. Had that been the foetus?

Distraught, I called my doctor. Yes, I had miscarried. "Make an appointment at the hospital for a D&C," she told me. But I had already passed the foetus. "You're going," she said. Liam was working and couldn't come with me so I headed to the hospital alone.

> *bleeding out my baby*
> *gobs*
> *of sadness pour*
> *from my eyes*
> *the tears*
> *from my sex*
> *the child that wasn't.*

I lay on a stretcher in an empty corridor, afraid, ashamed and confused. I could not remember ever feeling so low. I actually wanted to die. The stretcher was parked near a window and I turned my head to look out at the city's lone mountain. There, in my direct line of vision was the Mount Royal Cross. It is a giant thing, more than 100 ft tall, and now its power stood before me, seemingly alive and emanating love and compassion.

Good-bye you little nobody.

Liam and I held each other that night. For me, it was an intense yet brief period of grief because after bawling my eyes out I found myself feeling relieved. The miscarriage had been a reality check. *I was wrong.* I was not in control. I could not force my own destiny. I was not called to give birth to the next Saviour of the World. The truth hit me again:

> *You must face your fear of being who you are.*
> *Otherwise you will die.*
> *You will die alive.*

Who was I? An alcoholic and an addict. The long stretches of forced abstinence and failed attempts at "moderation" had proved it time and time again. My soul was dying. It was April, 1999, two months after the miscarriage and two years after my spiritual awakening in Edmonton. The mental insanity generated by endless attempts to control the obsession to drink and get high had peaked. In desperation, I sought help from a friend who was recovering from her own addictions and managing to stay clean with ongoing support. Reaching out to her changed my life.

> *I want to be at peace with myself. O help me God.*

ARE YOU CALLED?

YOU ANOINT MY HEAD WITH OIL;
MY CUP RUNS OVER.
GOODNESS AND MERCY SHALL FOLL
ALL THE DAYS OF MY LIFE;
ND I WILL DWELL IN THE HOUSE
OF THE LORD
F O R E V E R.

Getting off booze and dope with a network of sober support brought my year-long relationship with Liam to an agonizing end. I loved him to death but knew that if I stayed with him I wouldn't make it. The loss of our loving was somehow made bearable by the fact that I'd finally set my spirit free. Enough killing myself already! Moving back in with Jessica and focusing on healing gave me something I don't think I'd ever really had before: hope.

I can feel my higher power inside me.

I began to pray and meditate and cultivate a relationship with this "Higher Power," a term that was fairly new to me. It wasn't about believing in God, per se, but about believing that I wasn't God and I did not have the ability to control my addiction with willpower. Nurturing the idea that I could actually rely on the forces of the Cosmos to guide me, empower me, and transform my thinking, kept me sober.

Life began to change but not always in the prettiest way. Becoming more conscious meant attending to an inner well of unexpressed anger, fear and resentment. I had never really liked people. But I am a people! Liking myself was a foreign concept. I didn't know that my harsh judgment of others was really about me. I didn't know that my intolerance of other people's behaviours was connected to my inability to accept my own human imperfections.

Spiritual practice became integral to my well-being. I got serious about yoga and meditation. I shaved my head. I was no longer praying in secret. Prayer became a lifeline. "Look for the coincidences," a sober friend said. "Keep your eyes and your ears open for the spiritual messages. The Universe is listening."

Ah, this life. So beautiful. So hard. I am human. I do not want to escape myself.

Jesus continued to show up. While in Calgary for a theatre-training lab, I attended a gathering in a church basement where I met a man named Joseph. He wore a large cross around his neck and greeted me with a warm handshake. His eyes were crinkly and kind and he had a jolly smile that made me feel loved, even though we were strangers. Joseph gave most of his time to a soup kitchen run by the church and he talked about the marginalized people he served as though each of them were Jesus himself. Joseph emphasized this point by showing me a series of drawings of all the regulars who came to the kitchen for their daily bread. Their sunken, scarred and often smiling faces had been lovingly sketched in pencil and pencil crayon by a street artist and they now lined every square inch of the basement walls. Each portrait bore the same title: *The Face of Jesus*.

Jesus disguised as the forgotten ones from the soup-kitchen community? My journals tell tales of encounters I'd had with people living on the streets over the years, people whose lives touched mine and whose lives, in turn, I tried to touch. This notion of Jesus dwelling in the hearts of the downtrodden and downcast made sense to me and the chance meeting with Joseph and the technicolour portraits felt prophetic.

> *Why are we not taught to spread love and to be an instrument of peace when we are born?*

Back in Montreal, just a few months after the Jesus encounter in Calgary, I was given the opportunity to be of service to another kind of social outcast: the old person. I got a job in a private nursing home providing companionship for the residents, a situation that actually came about because of a coincidence that had taken place two years earlier: In the fall of 1998, on a dark and wet evening in Westmount, I had been waiting for a bus when a friend from theatre school had appeared at the same stop. We'd exchanged greetings and then he'd explained he had just come from the adjacent seniors' home where he coordinated a weekly play-reading group for the residents. After telling me a little bit about the gig and seeing my enthusiasm, he'd asked me if I'd be interested in taking over his job. I'd said yes and soon discovered a natural aptitude for being with elderly people. One of the residents, a Scottish lady named Lois, whose readings of the various characters were rich and full of intention, had become a beloved favourite of mine. Her friend, Mina, also Scottish, used to elbow Lois to remind her when it was her turn to read and Lois would elbow Mina right back, twice as hard. They were a riot.

Lois is the reason I ended up getting the job in the private nursing home two years later in the summer of 2000, not long after my return from Calgary. One day, Lois did not show up to the play-reading group. I remember feeling dread. Had she died? No, I was told her Alzheimer's had progressed to a point where she needed more care and had been moved. Alzheimer's? I'd just thought Lois was deaf. I vowed to go and see her.

The place where Lois was now living was a grand old mansion, now re-purposed as a privately-run, 12-bed nursing home. The door was locked, and when a Filipina aide answered, she told me to please watch for residents trying to get outside on my way out. She pointed me upstairs to Lois' bedroom and I found Lois lying on her bed with her black patent purse tucked under her head like a pillow. As I approached the bed I heard a "hello" from behind me.

"I'm Roberta, Lois' friend. I'm just sorting through her clothes, getting rid of what she doesn't need." I introduced myself and explained how much I'd missed Lois.

"She's a delight to be around," I told Roberta.

"Would you be interested in spending some more time with her? I could pay you," Roberta said.

At this point in my life I was very underemployed and pretty much living on faith. Odd jobs brought in enough to pay the rent but money was scarce. Being a starving artist in Montreal wasn't that hard because rent was cheap but I was eating a lot of bagels to stretch my pennies. Roberta's offer was nothing less than Impeccable Timing. (Look for the coincidences.)

After a short time, the owner of the nursing home asked me if I'd like to start spending time with Marie as well. Marie had Parkinson's, a good mind, and was lonely. Next, I was asked if I'd like to spend time with Marion. Marion had been a journalist and needed intellectual stimulation. She wanted to write a book. Then I was offered the "five-to-eight" shift in the evening, which involved feeding and toileting and helping the residents to bed. The idea terrified me. Emotional intimacy I could handle. The intimacy of bodily functions (and lack of function), not so much.

"I think I'm a better companion," I told the owner.

"Well, I disagree," she said, but didn't push me. Soon enough, however, the "five-to-eight" was back on the table. By that time my fear had dissipated and the next thing I knew I was working 30 hours a week as a personal support worker.

Washing Marie's feet I am in a state of grace.

Being a PSW is hard on the body but what I found even more difficult than the physical labour was the task-oriented nature of the work. Personal care doesn't always leave time for attending to the residents' emotional needs. "We gotta keep moving, Celia," was a common refrain from my shift partner whenever we had to get people fed or on the toilet or into bed. Handling the body and not the person inside didn't make sense to me. It took more time but so what? But the practical aspects of the job had to get done by the end-of-shift. It was tough.

Working with the elderly and the dying altered the way I experienced the world. It is so profound to spend time in the presence of a person whose body has become frail and useless, a person whose mind has become garbled and confused. I became more and more grateful for my mobility and well-running systems. I could walk, I could run, I could feed myself, I could wipe myself. I was independent, young and free. So had these residents been, once. If I didn't die young, I would become dependent on others for my well-being, too, one day.

C*herish this body. Cherish this life.*

"Maybe *this* is my calling," I thought, "Maybe I'm not supposed to pursue the life of a theatre artist at all." But then, out of the blue, I got a phone call from the Stratford Festival of Canada offering me a new play commission. That career miracle coincided with an equally exciting offer from a Toronto theatre company inviting me to join their Playwriting Lab.

My parents had just bought a house in Port Hope, only an hour away from Toronto (and two hours from Stratford). My father's work had moved them to the States in 1997, but they'd bought the house in Port Hope in 2001, thinking they would soon be moving back to Canada. The house was sitting empty, causing them some anxiety. I offered to look after it for them. They agreed. I left Montreal, and Lois, and all the beloved residents of the nursing home. Not without regret or sorrow but I was going where I was summoned.

In October 2001, less than a month after the world had been rocked by the terrorist attacks, I arrived in Port Hope. I went from living with two of my sisters in a cozy apartment in urban Montreal to living alone in an enormous house in small town Ontario. Kind of surreal.

Most folks could not believe I was the sole occupant and asked if I ever got scared living in such a big place all by myself. "Only sometimes," I'd say. Those times would occur after I'd turned out all the lights and was heading upstairs to bed. Walking up the the grand staircase in the dark, I would be seized by the image of a stranger grabbing me from behind. To control my terror, I'd slowly recite a section of the 23rd Psalm, saying, "The Lord is my Shepherd, I shall not want. Though I walk through the valley of the shadow of death, I will fear no evil, for thy rod and thy staff they comfort me." I didn't even know if I had the words right but the recitation would calm my nerves and remove the fear.

Playwriting became my primary focus and into my plays I channelled my deep concern for the state of the world and my gratitude for the privilege of my situation. Through my characters, I tried to work out my response to the political turmoil and the ongoing personal turmoil of my own human be-ing. One of my plays had a nun struggling with addiction as its main character. I was sober but contending with a low-grade depression that came and went.

My secondary focus was visiting Granny Jayne and Jack, my maternal grandparents, who lived only a short walk away. I went to see them once a day, every day, even if it was just to pop my head in the door. Most days I would sit with them and chat, asking them questions about their respective pasts, families and philosophies. Jack, a good doctor who lived with anxiety and depression, instilled a "never, ever, ever give up" spirit into his daughters and so into us. Granny Jayne, also a depressive, had been an opera singer whose career had been hampered by her low self-esteem. The three of us became close and this meant the world to them, and me.

"You make us remember our lives," Jack said to me one day, with tears in his eyes.

In the same way that I'd been struck by a desire to start jogging in Edmonton, I was now feeling an overwhelming urge to start singing. I had sung in a choir in Grade 7 but quit the following year when I'd turned cool. (At the end of Grade 8 the choir director wrote on my report card that she was sorry I'd quit and that the choir had missed me. I remember being totally surprised and truly saddened by her comment.) I began to look for opportunities to sing in Port Hope and one arrived while having tea with my grandparents and a friend of theirs named Helen.

"Come and sing in our choir," she said, "We'd love to have you."

Helen attended an Anglican church and the idea of joining her held some appeal. I'd accompanied one of the residents of the Montreal nursing home to Anglican services and had enjoyed the singing and the prayers. Helen brought me to church the following Sunday and the next thing I knew I was wearing a red robe with a poofy white collar and belting out Handel's *Messiah* with a group of happy, middle-class Protestants.

I loved singing the hymns but the rest of the service would bring up mixed emotions. Loud mental protests would set off running when Jesus was referred to as the *literal* son of God; the Loyalist flag mounted on the wall reproduced painful images I'd seen while living in Ireland of the Orangemen inciting sectarian violence by parading their righteous banners through the Catholic neighbourhoods; any mention of sin resurrected the old punishing God.

Yet some of the rituals had the opposite effect, inwardly electrifying the part of me that had been praying to God in secret for so many years. When the priest would say, "Lift up your hearts," I would lift my heart skyward and feel it full and brimming. The melodious chanting of "Lord have Mercy, Christ have Mercy" intoxicated me. Because I had never been baptized, I was invited to receive a blessing from the priest instead of the Eucharist (the wafer that becomes Christ's body by the priest's consecration rite). This meant that when the congregation would approach the altar to receive the bread of Holy Communion, I was supposed to cross my arms over my chest, indicating my unbaptized status. It didn't occur to me that this was unfair or unjust, and the priest's waxy finger drawing a cross upon my forehead secretly thrilled me.

As I opened myself further to Christianity, its conflicting teachings would often bar my way. I had volunteered and been matched with Star, a Little Sister from the local Big Brothers/Big Sisters organization, who attended the Baptist church and invited me to come with her one Sunday. Despite my lingering fear (Baptists were somehow more Jesus-freaky than Anglicans), I went with her. The service was lively and fun and I remember thinking, "These Baptists are actually alright!" but the closing announcement about the anti-gay marriage meeting after the service quashed my enthusiasm. Star then gave me a little silver cross with red gems on its points and, at first, I could not bring myself to wear the necklace. Too many judgments—my own and the projected ones of others. But I wanted Star to know I loved her and appreciated her gift, and the cross had shown up for me at one of my lowest points so … my fear got put aside and the pendant went around my neck.

I am learning how to let go absolutely.

In 2003, with the production at Stratford behind me, I used some of my royalties to do a month-long Yoga Teachers Training Course at the Sivananda Ashram on Paradise Island, Bahamas. I'd been introduced to the Sivananda organization while living in Montreal and had attended many classes in their Centre so I was prepared for the devotional lifestyle, the meditation and chanting, the difficult poses and mind-bending lectures, but it was my first real experience of living in community and I found the close-knit living with multiple personalities challenging. Yogic Philosophy, however, resonated. "God is One, the names are many," reads the sign at the ashram's entrance. I couldn't argue with that. And the idea that God was, in fact,

Consciousness itself made perfect sense to me. How could human beings have consciousness if the Condition of Our Existence wasn't also conscious?

My studies taught me that I am a bhakti yogi, one who desires to self-realize through devotion to God. I loved the learning and with all the *pranayama* (breath practice) and *asanas* (physical postures) and meditation and study, I began to feel as though my own conscious mind was expanding beyond its normal boundaries. I wasn't the only one: a woman in the course had some kind of a break with reality and had to be sent home. When I encountered her in the communal bathroom the night before her departure, our eyes met and we held each other's gaze with a deep recognition that said we both somehow mutually understood that she had not had a break with Reality at all. She had awakened to It.

During one of our classes, as I looked and listened to one of the Swamis giving a talk, I saw myself transformed into the Swami who was speaking, as if I were seeing the future of my life, who I would become, manifesting directly before my eyes. *I am that.*

I felt scared. Was I supposed to become an actual monk? Did I have to give up my life and live on an ashram and renounce the world?

> *The loss of what that would mean ... the gain no doubt but ... my intuition tells me I will be a swami. NO! NO! I don't want it. It's too much, it's too hard, I can't do it, I can't let go, I want a normal life, I want to be able to*

choose and I feel so sad, so so sad, so scared.
Help me GOD.

I took my fear to the Swami who'd been teaching us *The Bhagavad Gita*, the early Hindu scripture about Arjuna, a warrior who learns from Krishna (God) what it means to submit to one's prescribed duty. Swamiji (a familiar way to address a Swami) told me that if my response to the inner call had been that strong of a "no," then it wasn't really a call. Though her words comforted me, they didn't totally ring true and I sought further advice from one of the ashram's guest speakers, a Catholic Sister who had made herself available for support. In a candid conversation beneath the shade of a palm tree, I told the Sister that my curiosity about Christ was ever-deepening. Throughout the training, my eyes had been drawn more to the portrait of Jesus on the ashram temple's altar than to the other gods and gurus. She told me about her journey as a consecrated woman, describing silence as "a way of life" and explaining that "the vow of chastity comes from within." She also told me that "call" was something to be taken seriously and to pray for guidance.

"Is it possible to achieve self-realization and still enjoy love, relationships and money?" I asked Swamiji during one of the *Gita* classes, determined to find out if I could avoid renouncing my whole life.

"You don't get it!" she yelled. Have you ever been yelled at by a monk? It's not a good feeling. Shame seeped in, blood rushed to my face. The whole class got quiet. Then, she softened. "More and more you will receive … the more you let go of."

> *Lord, if you would have me become a Swami,*
> *I will do it. I will do whatever you will for me.*
> *I am yours. Take me. Make me who you desire*
> *me to be. Wholeheartedly, unreservedly, I give*
> *myself to you.*

As we neared the end of our training, our group was waiting to be called one-by-one into the temple for the initiation of our personal mantra. I noticed that Cindy, one of my fellow trainees, was smiling and walking toward me. She and I had been living in community for nearly a month but we'd barely spoken before now.

"I've been wanting to thank you for asking the un-askable question in class the other day," she said, referring to my embarrassing inquiry about self-realization and material pleasures. "You really took a bullet for all of us, you know that? There wasn't one person who didn't want to know the answer to that question."

"I've been struggling to make sense of my life," I told her. Cindy began to share about her own journey of letting go of control and not driving the bus of her life. Her language made me wonder if she was in recovery from addiction.

"I'm 25 years sober," she said, after I asked. Immediately, I burst into tears.

"I've been sober for four years," I said.

"Oh, baby," she said, and took me in her arms. There was no need to explain to her why I was bawling. I barely knew myself. She just knew, and rocked me.

Later that day, I was stopped on the way to dinner by an outspoken, intelligent yogi who'd brought attention to himself in many of the lectures by asking hard questions and arguing points with some of the teachers.

"Hey, didn't you say you're a performer?" he asked me. His voice sounded strained. "I've got laryngitis and I was supposed to emcee our talent-show graduation celebration. Would you be able to do it for me?"

With only a short time to prepare, I wrote a bit of yoga stand-up and a few little ditties to flesh out the bits between the acts. Very much at ease on stage and doing my best to shine my light, the evening came off without a hitch. The next morning, I overheard two women talking in a tent adjacent to mine. They didn't realize I was there and were quietly showering me with praise.

"Could you believe Celia last night? Wasn't she amazing?"

"I know! I had no idea she was so talented. She was really in her element."

This affirmation of my artistic, creative self felt like my answer. I didn't have to become a Swami. I could go home and continue to be a theatre artist.

Before leaving, I was given the spiritual name Mirabai, chosen especially for me by Swamiji after she witnessed my talents on stage. She told me Mirabai was a poet, a songstress and a mystic who was born into a wealthy family in the 16th C.

"She renounced all she had to follow Krishna," Swamiji told me, "and I know you love Krishna, so … it fits."

God is a process.

PART TWO

WAKING UP

MONK-EY MIND

A bout a month after I got back from the ashram I traveled back to the Yukon to work with a theatre company in Whitehorse on a new play development project. The artistic director and I had been at the National Theatre School together and we'd run into each other on the street in Montreal the previous summer. He knew I was from the Yukon and promised to find a way to bring me back up. At the end of the new play development project, he invited me to join the company as playwright-in-residence. At the time (spring 2003), moving back to the Yukon did not have huge appeal. But a year later, in the spring of 2004, Stratford had not invited me back, the Toronto company where I'd been developing a play declined to produce it, and my parents were getting ready to sell the house that had been my temporary haven. All roads led back to Whitehorse.

By the fall of 2005, I had settled into life as a Yukon theatre artist, co-founding Sour Brides Theatre with Moira Sauer, a good friend I'd met years before in Montreal. The company was thriving but the call to become a monk had not entirely left me. Often the internal nudging was quiet. Other times, it got very loud: renounce your worldly possessions, detach from your desire for a romantic relationship, enter a monastery. If I didn't do these things, I wondered, was I a complete failure in the spiritual life? Ignoring God's will for me? Living a selfish, self-centred, self-indulgent existence?

I also began to explore Christianity with more serious intention. Less judgmental and more curious about the teachings of Jesus, I began attending the

Whitehorse United Church, where the minister was a pregnant, divorced and re-married woman, which impressed me. Books by Christian writers like Emmett Fox and Florence Scovel Shinn introduced me to a New Thought approach (metaphysics, positive thinking, etc.) and showed me that there were just about as many versions of Christianity as there were Christians.

This more relaxed attitude led me to open the door, and welcome inside, a couple of fresh-faced, earnest young men in formal suits announcing themselves as belonging to The Church of Jesus Christ of Latter-day Saints. I'd come a long way, baby.

As they sat across from me on the couch and we talked about Jesus and service and love, I wondered if these boys, who looked like all-American football players, really believed anything they were telling me. They didn't skip a beat when I asked about their church's position on homosexuality. "We welcome them fully," one of them said. When pressed, however, they admitted that realigning a gay person's God-given sexuality to its proper orientation (aka straight) was the ultimate goal. Discouraged by their homophobia, I tossed their gift-copy of the Book of Mormon into the dumpster and asked Nature to forgive me for wasting the paper.

The Catholic religion's homophobic teachings were no better, but I knew Catholics who were gay and proud. I was getting to know Catholicism through a good friend I'd made named Sue, a staff worker at Mary House, a field house of the Madonna House Apostolate, a Roman Catholic organization run by both laypeople and priests, who live a "promised" life and are devoted to serving the poor. Sue had taken the MH promises of poverty, chastity and obedience and when I asked her if she wanted to go camping with me she'd said, "I'd love to but I have to ask permission." Austerity practices aside, Sue was totally down-to-earth. Catherine Doherty, the Foundress of Madonna House, had encouraged all her apostolates to be authentically themselves, and Sue, an Irish-Italian from New York, would say things like, "I'm out of my fucking mind and I'm going to fucking kill myself." We got along great.

The first time Sue came over to my minimally-furnished and sparely-decorated apartment she told me I lived like a Trappist monk. When I shared about my calling she said, "Oh, you definitely have a vocation." She encouraged me to get a spiritual director for the development of my formation. All of these terms were new to me. Sue also told me that if I was looking for an ego-smashing experience then living in community was the way to go. When she shared that the Madonna House apostolates beg for everything they have, I said, "Don't say beg," wanting her to use a more positive word.

"But it is begging. We literally beg for all our possessions. It's part of our poverty." That explained the conspicuous clothing style of their staff: thrift store chic.

Even though I was attending the Whitehorse United Church and participating in the community, there was always a feeling of not really belonging because I didn't really "believe." I was a bit of a church-hopper and started attending Quaker Meeting, an unorganized, sparsely attended hour of silent worship followed by a social tea. The Society of Friends, as Quakers are known, and their commitment to silence and social justice appealed to me. I also tried a couple of non-denominational Christian services but found them to be too evangelical. One church-hop took me to Marsh Lake, a small community outside of Whitehorse, for an afternoon summer service but no one else showed up. A local told me they didn't meet in the summer but the minister lived up the road so why not go straight there? Only in the Yukon.

As I pulled up to a cabin overlooking the lake where I'd spent many summers as a child, the minister, a woman with a brush-cut and dressed in a t-shirt and jeans, greeted me with a big smile and invited me to sit by a roaring campfire with her and her female partner. As the fierce heat from the flames rose above us, thickening the air and distorting the view of the treetops, we chatted about God and the church and finding a place to belong. I recounted the story of the ashram and described the call in my heart. This minister, who had known me for less than an hour, got quiet and then turned to me slowly and said, very plainly, "Celia, you already are a monk."

The book should end here, really. It was that simple. And I knew, at a very deep level, that she was right. But knowing something and living from that knowledge are two very different things.

> *I do have a hunger for you, GOD. I do have a hunger to serve you. Let me do so in every breath. Not wait for monk-hood. But now. In every single breath.*

For the next three years I worked non-stop. As a self-employed artist I was driven by a desire to succeed at my craft and to pay my monthly bills. I never knew where the money was going to come from and it was always feast or famine. At one point I was working on five different contracts as well as trying to co-run a theatre company and make short films.

Sometimes the body will stop us if we can't stop ourselves and in early 2007 a small patch of blisters erupted on my upper back. A visit to a clinic told me I had shingles and when I asked the nurse why, she told me there were three possible reasons for contracting the virus: being elderly (I was 36); compromised immune system (nope); stress. Hm. Stress? What *is* stress? I wasn't stressed out. Was I? Well, maybe. I'd just written, co-produced and starred in a short film with my sister Clara while doing all my other jobs. Did that qualify as stress?

For the first time in my life I realized that I had no idea how to stop, let alone rest. A vacation is a foreign concept for a self-employed person. We don't think we can afford to take time off, either financially or time-wise. But what I really needed was a *spiritual* vacation. Not a hotel room with a TV but a place where I could retreat from the world and go deeper. Going back to the ashram was too far and the cost was too high. The Yukon held little promise for something guided. Since Vancouver is Whitehorse's closest hub, it occurred to me to google "spiritual vacation British Columbia." What popped up? *Be Still and Know that I am God.*

When I clicked on those prophetic words (which, I later learned, come from Psalm 46: "God is our refuge and strength/an ever-present help in trouble"), I found a three-day silent retreat at the Naramata Centre in BC's Okanagan Valley. There was no hesitation.

Naramata is a little village nestled amongst vineyards and orchards climbing up and down desert hills. The Centre's pale green and brown low-lying buildings merge with the wild sage and pine-treed landscape. A labyrinth has been carefully crafted amidst peaceful gardens overlooking the lake, and the Chalmers Chapel, a post-and-beam design built in the shape of a giant fish, sits beneath a tremendous weeping willow. On my first visit inside, I felt immediately embraced by the Spirit. The space was holy and quiet. Giant beams made from recycled trees criss-crossed the ceiling and wooden crosses framed soaring, peaked windows. Hanging in the chapel's lighted alcove was a hand-sewn wall tapestry with a more progressive version of the Lord's Prayer stitched into the border. It took me a moment to notice the gauzy face of Jesus subtly quilted into one of its corners and staring quietly out at me.

"Okay, Jesus," I whispered to the iconic image, "You want me? Show up."

And show up Jesus did. When I walked into the Centre's Mustard Seed bookstore the very first thing I saw was a book with a photograph of the Christ the Redeemer statue on its cover. My only reference to the statue was a terrible film from the early eighties called *Blame it on Rio* that I had watched with one of my best friends in Grade 8. I remember three things from the movie: a very young Demi Moore appearing topless, her long hair covering her breasts, a fifty-year old Michael Caine having inappropriate sex with a seventeen-year old girl, and the Jesus statue, twelve stories high, overlooking the city of Rio de Janeiro. "Does that giant Jesus really exist?" I'd wondered.

The book, *Jesus: Uncovering the Life, Teachings and Relevance of a Religious Revolutionary*, by Marcus Borg, a Christian scholar, rocked my world. Jesus came *alive* for me. Not the Jesus born of a virgin but a historical Jesus, a Jew (who knew?), a mystic, a healer and a radical who preached against the domination systems of his time. A man who understood God as Intimate Reality. Borg's argument for a "more-than-literal" interpretation of Bible stories relieved me of having to care about whether they actually happened. This was a form of Christianity I could get on board with.

Journal entries from that time show that the monastic question continued to burn:

> *Why would I be given artistic ability only to*
> *live in cloistered silence?*

I needed guidance. Our facilitator, coincidentally named Lois, provided retreatants with spiritual direction and for the first time I got to experience the gift of having someone accompany me on my spiritual journey. A spiritual director is like a therapist for the soul, someone who listens deeply and, without actually directing anything, leads the directee back to herself. I brought to Lois my questions and doubts and fears about

God, vocation, love and suffering. In those first sessions, she helped me to discover the Merciless Taskmaster, the part of me effectively driving many of my achievements and much of my success but also not letting me or anyone else off the hook. It felt like I was being strangled by the Merciless Taskmaster's relentless perfectionism and self-criticism. Lois engaged my imagination, guiding me to dialogue with this rigid character, and we ended up doing an exercise where I pried the Taskmaster's hands away from my throat.

Despite my alignment with Borg's Jesus, I still didn't feel Christian and resisted making a commitment or belonging to a church. Having become used to crossing my arms to receive a blessing rather than the Eucharist at the Anglican church in Port Hope, I was still crossing my arms at the Whitehorse United Church despite the minister's repeated invitation for *everyone* to receive Holy Communion. "Everyone is welcome at the table," she'd say. But something about it felt wrong somehow. Eat the flesh of Jesus? It was unthinkable. (Apparently, his disciples had the same reaction.) The act of doing so made me think of a line from Shakespeare's *Hamlet:* "My gorge rises at it." It wasn't that it grossed me out, it was more that it seemed … *too* sacred. Taboo. Like, are you sure we're *allowed* to be doing this?

In the fall of 2008, I returned for another silent retreat at the Naramata Centre, this time for eight days. Much had happened in the interim: My sister Clara and I had made a second short film together in Paris, where she lived, and Sour Brides was now touring my play *So Many Doors*. I'd learned to slow down a little bit, and prayer and meditation had continued to change me, but workaholism was still my go-to and the desire for success continued to motivate my actions. I'd also been to a sex therapist to sort out my sexuality because I was finally admitting that I'd always been attracted to both men and women but had never come to terms with it. I'd only ever been in relationships with men, but I'd had drunken sex with women and was now considering same-sex dating. Therapy brought me to the conclusion that I am a "heterosexual-identified bisexual" who sometimes practices celibacy for monastic purposes. Some people abhor labels but this one allowed me to relax and welcome a new man into my life, my first sexual relationship since the break-up with Liam, eight years earlier. Despite my willingness to explore real intimacy with my lover, he dumped me by email not long after saying "I love you." Apparently, I still knew how to pick 'em.

After the dumping, my heart was made lighter by the daily rhythm of walks, naps, spiritual direction with Lois, and silent meals during that second retreat at Naramata. Another myth-buster book called *Son of Man: The Mystical Path to Christ* by Andrew Harvey had jumped into my hands in the bookstore and, with it, another radical take on Jesus and what Harvey calls the Christ-Love. Like the Borg book, these notions were both a discovery and a recognition, seeming to expand and confirm my own experience of the Reciprocal Love of the Universe.

About four days into the retreat, I went for a hike, scrambling up a steep, ragged knoll to arrive at the edge of a clay cliff overlooking the lake. The sun was peeking through clouds and illuminating the far shoreline, a series of rocky tiers and low mountains with dark green veins. Standing on the edge of a cliff can produce in me an almost mad temptation to throw myself over the side. As I contemplated this idea, a noise turned me around. Not far away, where the hill flattened out, a stag was munching on some brush. He looked up and our eyes met. His face then transfigured and became the face of Jesus. I remember gasping. He then turned his head away and became a deer again, licking his lips and swallowing, contracting his round, white rump and pooping out a waterfall of black pellets. I took a step toward him and he leapt away.

As I made my way back to the Naramata Centre, I wondered at what I'd just seen. How had the face of Jesus appeared in the face of a deer? In the silence of the Chalmers Chapel, I set up a bed of cushions and lay down in front of the altar, the gauzy face of Jesus staring down at me. The pain of being dumped by my lover rose to the surface and I began to cry. My feelings of not being good enough, being unlovable, being unforgivable poured out with the tears. As the crying abated and the silence once more permeated the sanctuary, I heard a voice. Not my own, but in me, speaking to me and through me, as me but not me, from me but beyond me, yet closer, closer than anything:

> *Whenever you are hurt I am there to love you, when no one else loves you, I love you. I will never leave you. I am always with you and I love you, no matter what. No matter what, I love you.*

In my next session with Lois, I told her about seeing Jesus in the face of the deer and the inner voice of unconditional love that I'd heard in the chapel.

"Okay, so if I am loved *no matter what*, then there is nothing to forgive." Lois nodded. "But how do I *accept* unconditional love?"

"All you have to do is keep making space within you," she said. "Create that space for it to have a home inside you." The tears returned. Somebody had once told me that crying is healing. Well, bring it on. Lois agreed, apparently. "Just let it come out," she said. With her encouragement I allowed buried sounds in my body to come past my throat and into the room at full volume. She held the space and let me be just as I was, howling and blubbering like a madwoman. Eventually, I stopped.

"Is there anything, any gesture that needs to happen for you to celebrate the act of accepting that this gift of unconditional love is truly yours?" Lois asked. I closed my eyes and listened.

Go down to the water.

"I'm supposed to go jump in the lake," I told her. She tilted her head, not understanding. And then we started to laugh. Hysterically. "I don't have a bathing suit," I said, after we'd finally stopped laughing, but that set us off again.

"Let me find you a towel," Lois said, still giggling. She came out with a red bathmat and a cream-coloured blanket. "It's all I've got."

"Lake water in BC in November can't be any colder than river water in the Yukon in July," I said. "I just hope I don't get arrested." We cracked up again and I set off toward the beach. On the way, I passed a group of women doing a boot-camp-style work-out. "At least they're all women," I thought to myself, knowing I was about to get naked.

Arriving at the water's edge it occurred to me that I actually might be crazy. But something had just been healed in me and this was, apparently, the only way to honour it. Taking off my clothes, walking into the frigid water, enduring the pain in my feet from the rocks, I trusted the inner prompt and took a breath, plunging below the surface and immediately shooting back up like a rocket.

The girl who feels unworthy is re-born.

Back on shore, I dressed, shivering and elated. Gleeful and shining, on fire with happiness, the red-turban bathmat wrapped around my head and the creamy blanket covering me like a tunic, I passed the exercising women feeling like an early disciple, out of time and yet back in place. Joy was radiating from my frozen pores. The idea that I had been born-again suddenly struck me as hysterically funny and I laughed out loud.

I have received my baptism.

COMMON LIFE

fr putting pressure on me! some good pieces: you have to follow your con-science; go for a walk to re-center; return to my prayer-life as often as i can; we can only ever do the next step; temptation is everywhere & it esp. comes up when we make a decision from the Heart; embrace the world AND be detached from it, LOVE IT NOT WITH ATTACHMENT; don't talk too much with the family about the call because people cannot help with something they do not understand. ENJOY LIFE, GOD IS EVERYWHERE, KEEP PRAYING FOR PURITY OF THE HEART.

THE VOWS FORM A UNITY CIRCLING AROUND A CENTRAL AXIS

· CONVERSION · VOWS · · · CHASTITY · · POVERTY · OBEDIENCE · STABILITY ·

UNITY

TRANSFORMATION IN CHRIST

THE AXIS IS THE SPIRITUALITY FROM WHICH THE VOWS FLOW AND TO WHICH THEY ARE DIRECTED.

THE SPIRITUAL DIMENSIONS OF THE VOWS UNDERLIE THEIR MORE EXTERNAL OBLIGATIONS

FROM C.O.C. - SPIRITUALITY AND PROFESSION

conversatio = MANNER OF LIFE
politeia = RELATION OF CITIZEN TO BODY POLITIC; PERSONAL MANNER OF
        BEHAVIOUR; WAY OF LIFE; CITIZENSHIP; HOMELAND; COMMUNITY;
        MEMBERSHIP; CONDUCT; EVERYDAY LIFE.
- EACH MONK OR GROUP OF MONKS HAD HIS politeia, HIS PARTICULAR

In 2010, I received an email from the Naramata Centre inviting me to consider a two-year program called The Common Life. We would be a community of pilgrims, invited to give focused time and energy to discovering what it means "to take seriously Jesus' call to bring out the God-flavours and God-colours in the world today." The letter added that "God is not a secret to be kept. We're going public with this, as public as a city on a hill." How could I refuse such a call? After talking with the facilitator, Tim Scorer, a spiritual director and author who had collaborated on a study guide with Marcus Borg for his book *Jesus*, I registered, committing to six in-person sessions in Naramata every four months for the next two years.

On that first weekend, with seventeen of us and Tim sitting together in a circle, I suddenly felt that I'd made a big mistake. Despite the fact that the invitation had explicitly said we would be "going public with God," I could feel myself getting smaller and smaller as we went around the circle and each person spoke about their Christian lives. I did not belong here. "Run for the hills," fear said. "Get out of here." Instead, when it came to be my turn, I employed a tool I'd gained from doing inner work: tell on yourself.

"I wasn't raised Christian," I said to the group, "And talking about Jesus in public makes me feel extremely uncomfortable. But maybe I'm just another Jesus freak."

Everybody laughed. I managed to laugh, too, but I was really pretty bummed out. I didn't want to be like everybody else!

Those Common Life weekends were incredibly special. Tim Scorer's Christianity is so open, so inclusive and relaxed and he is so adept at leadership that our group bonded beautifully. Tim resists patriarchal language and, because of his work with Borg, subscribes to the "more-than-literal" interpretation of Scripture. He brought Bible stories alive through dramatic re-enactment, rooting their deeper meaning in our collective consciousness, like the morning he brought us all down to the lake at dawn to feed us fish he'd just cooked on a campfire. As the sun came up, Tim read a story from *The Gospel According to John* where the resurrected Jesus cooks fish for his disciples on a charcoal fire and invites them to come and have breakfast. Just like Jesus in the story, Tim took bread and gave it to each of us. *This* was Holy Communion.

Over the next two years, being part of Common Life reinforced my spiritual practices and helped me to playfully and gratefully celebrate the goodness of life *in community*. Allowing myself to be seen by others in a more transparent way deepened my self-acceptance. Surprise, surprise: I *am* just like everybody else! As I gained spiritual maturity, it began to dawn on me that despite my love for theatre and performing, my career had primarily been motivated by a need for outside approval. The more I let go of this need to be validated by others, the less desire I had to run a theatre company, and my life-focus turned more and more toward how I could share the spiritual journey with others.

During that time, I met and started dating a Swiss man named Rohlf, who'd been in the Yukon for many years. We met at Quaker Meeting and it sparked an attraction. He was kind and curious and I felt ready to explore a romantic relationship again.

With eyes on a new career, I took a training course for coaching, attended Toastmasters to develop professional speaking skills and created workshops for personal growth. I branded my business *Inspiring Works*. My yoga training had taught me to teach what I know so *Walk Through Your Fear* and *Being Enough* became my trademarks. Mistakes occurred: in one of my workshops a woman accused me of pushing propaganda when I included a question about a Higher Power in a writing exercise. Successes happened, like first prize in the Toastmasters' International Speech Contest. There seemed to be enormous potential in me and in what I was doing but the big break just wasn't happening fast enough. Money was tight and I needed a paying job.

In the spring of 2012, I started substitute teaching in the Whitehorse school system. In the fall, I started a full-time job as an Educational Assistant (EA) in a classroom for students with special needs. I loved the work and adored the student I was assigned to spend time with each day. She and her fellow students, who lived with such intense physical and intellectual challenges, began to teach *me*. From them, I gained further insight into the true meaning of humility as my patience was constantly being tried. Sometimes, when my frustration had got the better of me, I would whisper to the students, "I'm not doing very well, am I?" Happily, after 17 years of being self-employed, I was finally receiving a regular paycheque. Every two weeks, when the money would arrive into my bank account I'd think, "They're paying me *again*?"

That year, I applied to the Pacific Jubilee Program (PJP), an experiential (rather than academic), two-year spiritual direction training program where Lois was a co-facilitator and where she herself had completed her training years before. Two years of the Common Life program qualified as an equivalent to PJP's first year of training and I was able to join PJP in the second year of its program, which began and ended with an 8-day intensive at the Naramata Centre.

PJP also included an extensive reading list, a number of creative, responsive projects and the hands-on practice of spiritual direction. I suddenly had two "directees" to accompany on their respective spiritual journeys and my listening skills strengthened as did my ability to ask evocative questions rather than fix or solve a directee's problems. For accountability, I was required to have both a supervisor and a peer-supervision group. All of this inner work continued to expand my self-awareness and further teach me to keep trusting the Flow of Life, a necessary practice seeing as how I continued to live with an obsessive mind, fits of despair and ongoing anxious flutters.

It's worth mentioning, too, that the practice of Centering Prayer, a form of meditation that comes out of the Christian contemplative tradition, had newly become an important part of my days. Known as a "prayer of consent" and a receptive form of meditation, Centering Prayer is practiced by returning to a sacred word of my choice whenever I become engaged with my thoughts. The sacred word is a place holder, not a mantra, and is meant to be a symbol of my consent to the presence and action of God *within* me. Though I'd been meditating with my mantra from the ashram for many years, Centering Prayer fit me in a way the repetition of the mantra had not. I liked that I didn't have to do anything more than simply return to a sacred word when my thoughts hooked me, and I religiously began sitting twice a day, for 20-30 minutes at a time.

In terms of my relationship, Rohlf and I weren't a great match. I wanted to talk and he wanted to retreat. I suppose I could have just let him be but that old familial force of my grandfather Jack's dictum, "never, ever, ever give up," made me think I had to make it work. Despite an inner desperation to get out, I stayed in.

Rohlf had always wanted to live in community and though the idea was less foreign to me because of the Common Life program I wasn't convinced communal living was for me. "You are more individualistic," Rohlf told me. This felt like an insult considering all the service I was doing for others. In order to prove him wrong and make him happy, I got on board with his vision of sharing a common life with like-minded people in our future. I convinced myself I could do it even though I was happiest living alone.

In January 2013, after almost two years together, Rohlf returned to Europe to live in a monastery for three months, something he'd been longing to do for some time. Part of me was wounded by this but I focused on supporting his spiritual journey. We agreed that I would join him in Europe that July when school was out, and together we would explore different community-living options. But when spring arrived, Rohlf announced he had met another woman through the monastery. Though our relationship had not been easy, I was devastated by the rejection.

In a Skype conversation, I asked Rohlf if he wanted to go back to being friends. Hoping he would say no so I wouldn't have to deal with the thorns of failure and abandonment, I was stung when he enthusiastically agreed. We pressed "re-set" and he wrote to me soon after: "I am confident that we can unfold a relationship of mutual presence and collaboration without the romantic entanglements." Not me.

I was on tour in Ottawa in one of my final projects as a theatre artist and the burning pain of heartbreak sent me to a church around the corner. As I walked up the steps on that sunny May morning, I noted the name on the welcome sign: Saint Theresa Roman Catholic Church. I'd been introduced to St. Teresa of Avila only a week before, during the final PJP intensive, and noted the coincidence. I didn't yet know that the "h" in the name made it not St. Teresa of Avila but St. Thérèse of Lisieux, another mystic saint and giant in the contemporary contemplative movement whom I would soon encounter as well.

The priest's message that morning was about letting go. These were clear instructions from the Conscious Universe and the priest's homily released a torrent of disappointment and grief.

With my ticket to Europe already booked, I decided to re-jig my plans. I had been envious when Rohlf had first announced his decision to go and live in a monastery. Didn't I want to live in a monastery, too? Hadn't I been living with the question of my monk-hood for *ten years*?

Because there was no place in Europe I would rather be than Ireland, I searched "monastic retreat Ireland." I discovered Mount Carmel, a "Roman Catholic, ecumenical community of vowed men and women with roots in the Carmelite contemplative tradition." Carmelites, I learned, were a cloistered order so named for a group of desert hermits who lived on the actual Mount Carmel in (what is now) Israel in the earliest days of Christianity. Silence and contemplation were vital to their common life.

Mount Carmel's website showed a photo of a wooden plaque with the words *Be Still and Know That I am God* carved into it. This was all the evidence required to tell me this was the place. After a quick exchange of emails with Kit, one of the monks, my spot was secured. I would come for four weeks starting in early July and work part-time and pay half the price.

I'm. So. Excited.

Dublin had changed so much since I'd lived there in 1996. I'd been back for visits in both 2000 and 2008 but neither of those brief glimpses were of any help in navigating the city's face-lifted streets. When I stepped out of the hostel for a stroll on the summer evening of my arrival, I could not get my bearings. What I did recognize were the drunks and the beggars and the hucksters trying to make a living in the crowded city centre. These poor and forgotten ones had been even further displaced by the shiny new bridges and fancy glass structures of economic growth.

I managed to find the bus station the next morning and headed into the West. Something in my heart sings when I am back on Irish soil, and the view from the bus of the bright green fields and big-cloud sky brought back good memories and renewed my happiness.

At an unnamed stop beside a graveyard, I was picked up by Barb, a sexagenarian American dressed in blue jeans and a purple fleece jacket. Barb referred to herself as "the other monk" at Mount Carmel. I especially liked that these officially consecrated women called themselves monks instead of nuns. My interior calling had always said "monk" as opposed to "nun" but in the Christian tradition women don't really get to be called monks. This bothered me. But Mount Carmel was doing it differently!

On the short drive to the main house, Barb told me the story of how their religious order had inherited the property. She and Kit, the monk I'd corresponded with to organize my stay, currently lived with two laypeople, making Mount Carmel a whopping community of four souls.

"And that is Bull Mountain," Barb said, indicating a low-lying range of hills not far ahead of us.

"How close is the sea?" I asked.

"About three miles in the other direction. We have a bike you can use." As we drew nearer to Mount Carmel, Barb pointed to a series of tiny houses scattered throughout the farm fields and hillsides on either side of the road. "We built all of our hermitages," she said.

As we pulled in through the gate, the sign from the photo I'd seen on the website greeted us: *Be Still and Know that I am God*. Barb parked in front of the main house, a single-storey Georgian mansion made of grey stone and covered in dark-green ivy. We walked through sloping gardens past a wedge of forest to the hermitage where I would be staying. I could hear a fast-running brook behind the trees. The hermitage, a wee cottage in the middle of a field of wild-growing flowers and grasses, had a sign on the door that read "*Thérèse*."

"We name them after the saints," Barb said as she opened the door. The little house was spacious, with high ceilings and big windows, a desk, bed and window seat, and a corner kitchen and tiny bathroom. What more did a person need?

After Barb left, I explored the books on the desk: the writings of someone called St. John of the Cross, a heavy tome called *The Philokalia*, and a scrappy, used copy of *Mere Christianity* by C.S. Lewis, whom I at least recognized as the author of *The Lion, The Witch and the Wardrobe*. After skimming the books, I took off my hiking boots and sat outside on a small patch of mowed lawn beside the hermitage and listened to the birds and the mooing cows in the field behind the trees. I was officially in heaven.

I followed the rhythm of the community and found my own. Each day, I'd walk over to the chapel in the main house for Lauds in the morning and Vespers in the evening. Together we would pray the Divine Office, a communal prayer performed by most Christian religious orders, a kind of choral poetry-slam of the Book of Psalms. As a writer and lover of words, the psalms' poetic lamenting and rejoicing, their rhythmic play and repetition, hypnotized and seduced me. I began to memorize and recite them:

> *O all you works of the Lord; O bless the Lord ...*
> *To you be highest glory and praise forever.*

After Lauds, I would set down to the business of studying how to become a monk. I found a book in the monastery's extensive library called *Centered on Christ: A Guide to Monastic Profession* by Augustine Roberts, and began to devour it with all the fervour of a novice, copying out passages in my journal and contemplating "conversion of life."

> *The monk is not her own boss ...*

Afternoons, I would work in the garden, weeding or harvesting, whatever needed to be done. A weekly Desert Day, when nothing was scheduled but solitude, gave me time to meditate for longer periods and commune with nature. On these days, I would ramble over the grassy hills, searching for the 6000-year-old megalithic tombs I'd heard were scattered about and find them, marvelling at what stories must be held in their carefully calculated structures and dark crevices. Bike rides to the sea bought time to watch endless waves crash into the rocks with supreme force, knocking spray so high into the air it would make me laugh out loud.

The Catholic prayers and rigorous study were having a dual effect. On one hand, I was connecting to a history of words and worship that appealed to me. On the other, I was discovering some of the more rigid aspects of Catholic doctrine. These rules and regulations threatened to erode my love of Catholicism's more mystical rites.

> *I do not understand these mysteries and yet they speak to me. Why should Jesus speak to me? Why should the Christ make itself known to me? Why should Catholicism call to me?*

Always I would turn to the land for realignment. One morning, a sudden urge to tackle Bull Mountain sent me out of the hermitage and up the road to make the climb. Hopping a fence and making my way through the boggy field toward the incline, an enormous face appeared in the configuration of rocks about halfway up. I named her Mother of the Mountain and she began to speak through me in an Irish accent as I climbed:

> *When you rejoice in Creation, Creation rejoices. There is no separation. In that instant when you are rejoicing in the Lord (and by "Lord" I mean All That Is, All That Ever Was, All That Ever Will Be), there is only One.*

Once a week, the community would gather for Eucharistic Adoration, the act of sitting or kneeling together for an hour, or longer, if we desired, in silent contemplation of the Blessed Sacrament. The Blessed

Sacrament, the Catholics believe, is the "real presence" of Jesus abiding in the Host, or bread, which is not bread at all but a wafer made from unleavened dough. The Host has been consecrated by an ordained priest through the dual power of his speaking the Eucharistic Prayer and the descent of the Holy Spirit, sent by God from heaven. For Catholics, this combination of actions "transubstantiates" the bread into the actual Body of Christ and so it makes complete sense to them to place God in a decorative chamber (ironically named a monstrance) to be adored. To the rest of us, a whole hour spent staring at a wafer seems ludicrous. I could just see my father shaking his head. Adoration is, admittedly, deeply strange. But as I gave myself to the contemplative aspect, I found the practice strangely comforting. It was, for me, a time to give thanks and praise and to adore Life and all its mysteries.

There is nothing more important than this.

In the evenings, I created my own private ritual of adoration: a pilgrimage to the local cemetery a mile and a half away. After a simple supper of rice and beans and greens from the garden, I'd stroll along the country road, stopping to talk to a handsome donkey in one field and two pretty, cream-coloured cows in another. As I walked, I would notice what the clouds were doing and sometimes I could even taste the salt from the sea in the air.

Once inside the graveyard, I'd make my way past the lichen-covered and newly-polished stones, passing one that had the name Celia on it, reminding me that I was going to die one day. Then, with the sun nearly gone, I would kneel at the foot of a giant cross, my knees pressing uncomfortably into the small gravel stones, and pray. With the Bull Mountain in the distance, my prayers would go up to both the crucified figure hanging above me and to the big sky and green hills beyond.

Show me what to do ...

Kit was available for spiritual direction and I took advantage of it. For Catholics, vocational discernment is a given. If you say to a Catholic, "I think I have a calling," they will not say, "A what? What do you mean? That's crazy!" They will say, "What order are you thinking of joining?" Kit understood me immediately. She also said she could help me unpack my reservations.

"Let's look at them," she said.

"It's pretty much the usual top three," I told her, "the Virgin Birth, abortion and homosexuality." Kit nodded and talked a little bit about Mary and her "yes" to God.

"*Something* happened," she said, admitting that we didn't really know what that something had been. Regarding abortion she said it was just not right. "It's *life*," she insisted. (Do you kill mosquitos? I wanted to ask, because that's life, too. But don't be flippant, Celia.)

"What if a woman wanted to have an abortion but couldn't, because it was unavailable to her?" I asked Kit. "She'd have to go about it in a way that would put both her life and the life of the foetus in jeopardy.

Legalizing abortion isn't saying it's right. It's making it safe for women."

"You make a very good point," said Kit, "and I'm going to think about what you're saying."

I decided to leave the topic of homosexuality for another time and instead tackle the monk question. I also wanted to get clarification on whether it was permissible to receive Holy Communion.

"Have you been baptized?" Kit asked.

"Not by the church," I answered, and told her the story of my experience in Lake Okanagan.

"Baptism of desire," she said.

"What does that mean?"

"It means that your desire for baptism is what makes it legitimate."

She then gave me permission to receive the Eucharist and I gladly accepted. My gorge no longer rose at the idea of receiving and it now seemed novel, even exciting, to be able to participate in the ritual. Kit then tested me on the question of whether I was being called to become a monk.

"What does being a monk mean to you?"

"I think it means being entirely devoted to God. Living my life in total communion with God, and just … giving my whole life to God." She smiled.

"What?" I asked.

"You're romanticizing it," she said. "You need to live in community. Then you'll find out what it means when someone is driving you crazy and you just want to strangle them."

Kit's words brought back the words of my friend Sue from the Madonna House community, how communal life was actually an ego-smashing experience. My romantic illusions needed to be smashed by the real common life.

Day after day I would transcribe passages from *Centered on Christ* on conversion of life, living a life of selfless service, renouncing the world, committing wholly to humility, poverty, chastity, obedience, community. This good work was countered by the latest obsessions *du jour*: anger arising from the recent breakup with Rohlf, which took pages and pages of journalling to work through, and righteous judgments about Mount Carmel's privileged lifestyle. How could they be authentic when they lived in nice little homes with nary a poor person in sight?

"Everybody's poor, Celia," Kit had countered when I dared to bring up the question. There may have been some defensiveness in her response but the broader truth of what she was saying took hold.

"You mean because we're all dependent on God?"

"Yup," she said.

I pondered this idea that all humans are essentially poor because we are unable to sustain life ourselves. We are all reliant on this thing we call Life. It made sense but Lord, it's hard to be humble when your mind is a jumble of fear. My black-and-white thinking continued to tell me that following the call meant renouncing my paying job and leaving my lovely apartment and cat, Lukie. In short, everything.

Another book about monastic life highlighted a particular kind of religious person, a pious man who practices all kinds of observances but keeps God out of his life. *That's me*, I thought. *I am that person. I am faithful but I still want to do things my way.* I sensed that the contemplative life was really the only way, the only *really* satisfying way to live and yet because I was not willing to let go of my own worldliness, I was destined to live a kind of half life. After making this discovery, my journal entry records what felt like a desolating truth:

> *I am not willing to renounce my selfishness.*
> *In this way, a conversion of life is impossible.*
> *I am too selfish to become a monk.*

Famous last words.

YOU ARE CALLED

who are you
really, mary?
were you just
a child who
lived & bore a
child & we have
made you our
suffering Lady?
who are you
to yourself?

see an ancient wall from this window beside
ed. it is on the far side of the brook. who built
hat was its purpose? to line the edge of the
running by for a dwelling? for support? for
the line?   spoke of the walls lining

The next morning as I was getting dressed there was a knock on the hermitage door. I froze. No one comes to your hermitage door. Clad only in underwear and a t-shirt, I looked around for my leggings. Talk about being caught with your pants down. Another knock.

"May I come in?" Kit asked, as I cracked open the door. "So, how's it going?" she asked me, after I'd found my leggings and invited her to sit down. I told her about my crushing discovery, that I was too selfish to become a monk. "That's very interesting … in light of what I'm doing here." She paused. "Celia, I know this might sound crazy to you but I felt pulled by God to come here this morning. I feel you have been touched by God and I would like to invite you to come and live with us for a year."

Everything in my life converged in that one moment.

O, Lord, you have blessed me with a calling.

"I'm sorry to ruin your retreat," she said after we'd talked about what it all might mean. "No doubt there will be a million details for you to work out. Let us know what you decide."

My mind went into planning-overdrive. I would first continue my travels, then go back to the Yukon, sell the truck, sublet or let go of the apartment, find a home for Lukie the cat, quit the job and return to Mount Carmel in September. It occurred to me, however, that there were two teeny-tiny obstacles: I'd already committed to returning as an EA for another school year, and I'd promised myself I'd finish *Last Stop for Miles*, the feature film I'd shot the previous summer (about a woman who spirals into alcoholism after experiencing a brutal trauma).

That afternoon, I went for a run to quell the mental back-and-forth generated by Kit's invitation. Up ahead of me on the road I saw Margaret, an attractive, casually-dressed woman in her sixties with whom I'd connected briefly on the previous Sunday during the community meal. In a conversation that had touched on Dorothy Day, a famous journalist and convert to Catholicism who had "repented" her decision to have an abortion, Margaret's more liberal attitude had gotten my attention. She had said something about none of us being in a position to judge.

Seeing Margaret on the road felt like a Divine Prompt to ask for help and, after excusing myself for disturbing her walk, I told her Kit had invited me to come and live at Mount Carmel for a year and that I needed guidance. She immediately expressed her delight in assisting me and we arranged to meet later that day in the main house.

When I showed up in the waning afternoon she was putting the finishing touches on an altar of rocks and flowers in front of an old fireplace. Two chairs awaited us. Margaret then lit a candle and invited a time of silence. We sat across from each other in the greying light and said nothing for a good while. Rain began to splatter the glass of the tall windows and I shivered, wishing the fire was lit.

"Thank you for this," I finally said, "I just had an intuitive idea to ask you for help."

"It's not so strange, Celia," she said, informing me that she was not only a psychotherapist and spiritual counsellor but also a consecrated religious Sister. I thought she might have been a spiritual director but I never would have guessed she was a nun. Clearly, a book cannot be judged by its cover. I gave her an overview of my spiritual journey, ending with the story of Kit's knock on the hermitage door.

"I mean, the day after I admit I'm too selfish to become a monk Kit appears at my door with this invitation?"

"What do you make of it?" she asked.

"It feels like I really am being called."

"And what about this word 'selfish'? That's a very hard word."

"Being hard on myself is my default position," I sighed. "But isn't it selfish though? I don't actually want to give up my life for God. I want what I want. I don't want to sacrifice myself. That's selfish, isn't it? Not to mention I work with a beloved student and leaving my job would mean abandoning her. Leaving my cat. All my friends. My apartment."

"You do realize that there is long discernment process involved. One doesn't become a nun overnight. There is postulancy, novitiate, temporary profession, full profession …"

Right. I'd only been invited to come and live with the community for a year. I wasn't even Catholic! Still, even saying yes to living at Mount Carmel for a year would mean a major life change.

"I understand from a spiritual perspective that I can't make a mistake and yet I'm still afraid to make a mistake."

"Spirit is here," Margaret said. "And Spirit is in Canada. Spirit will not leave you. Spirit is with you whatever you do. Stay with your heart, your gut, whatever is true for you."

My sister Melissa once joked that I couldn't make a decision without checking with three people first. She wasn't wrong. A long-distance conversation with Lois came next.

"Imagine you are holding Mount Carmel in one hand and your life in the Yukon in the other," Lois offered through the phone lines, and I held my hands out in front of me, feeling the weight of each situation in the palm of each hand. "Which one feels like it has more pull?"

It was Mount Carmel. My heart was ready to submit. Nevermind my reservations. Nevermind what I still perceived to be a hypocritical, oppressive, rigid hierarchy. My love for certain aspects of the Catholic faith had grown exponentially. I thought of Mary's "yes" to God. The more-than-literal truth of that story was about an ultimate act of readiness. Her response, "Be it done unto me according to Thy word," was one of total obedience and humility. For Catholics, the "Mary yes" is the pinnacle of faith. Do not question, do not deliberate. If God asks, just say "yes."

The next morning after Lauds I approached Kit and Barb to tell them the good news. Just as I opened my mouth to speak, one of the community workers called Barb away and I hesitated, wondering if my timing was off. But Kit remained and I told her my decision. Her face darkened.

"I haven't talked to Barb about my proposal so if you could just hold tight until I do. I'll let you know." She went out. My gut tightened. Kit had asked me to come and live at Mount Carmel without consulting Barb?

"I'm upset that she would do that," Barb told me when she came to speak to me after Kit had talked with her. I learned from our conversation that things were not as they appeared. There was strife in the community, and over the next two weeks, more cracks began to show, and my confusion grew. This time I consulted Dympna, a fellow guest and Sister, with whom I'd formed a friendship. Dympna had taught me about the namesake of my assigned hermitage, Saint Thérèse of Lisieux, also known as the Little Flower. Saint Thérèse's path of humility and innocence was known as her "Little Way" and it was a Way worth following.

"You are a contemplative," Dympna said, when I told her what was happening. "But you must remember that it is your life you are discerning, not a place."

Dympna's words stayed with me as my retreat came to an end and I prepared to head back across the pond to take care of the million details. So did the advice of another guest with whom I'd shared my story:

"Patience is the gift of the Holy Spirit," that guest had told me. "God is in the waiting."

The good-bye with Kit and Barb was filled with uncertainty. Would I return in just a few weeks time to begin an adventure with them? I left my hiking boots and a sweater there, certain that I would.

"We'll see what happens!" Kit said, as she hugged me and put me on the bus back to Dublin. I was grateful for my seat-mate, a young woman who'd also been on retreat at Mount Carmel during my last week. She wanted to talk about her troubles and it took my mind off the tangled web of my own spinning thoughts.

As the bus pulled in to the Dublin airport I noticed for the first time that there was a church right beside the terminal. How many times had I been to the Dublin airport? Half a dozen? Never had I noticed it before. Airport chapels tend to be sanitized prayer rooms relegated to some remote corner of the furthest-away building. Only in Ireland would there be an actual bricks-and-mortar structure with daily Mass times and an on-site priest. Of course I had to go, and with time to spend (after giving up my seat for an easy 200 Euro when the flight was overbooked), I could meditate and then make the one o'clock Mass.

A stone sculpture of Mary greeted me as I entered the courtyard of Our Lady Queen of Heaven. There she was, standing in the courtyard, her head tilted toward the sky and her arms wide open, lifting up the suffering of the world. Inside, I took a seat beside a woman who'd spread devotional cards and rosaries all around and in front of her. The Catholic faith is so sure of itself, I thought. It knows exactly what it is. It has answers and it promises certainty. I was looking for certainty.

When the airport priest delivered the homily, he told us it was the feast day of another Teresa, Saint Teresa Benedicta of the Cross, also known as Edith Stein, a Jew who converted to Catholicism and became a Carmelite nun. She suffered at the hands of the Nazis in Auschwitz and died in the gas chamber on August 9, 1942, this very day. Then the priest looked directly at me and said, "What the world needs is more contemplatives."

Didn't this seal the deal? Kit knocking on my hermitage door had been my Jesus-knocking-at-the-door moment. Do you know the image? Jesus, illumined by the light from his lantern or his halo or his heart or the distant sky, stands at a door with his fist held up, poised to knock. The message of this popular picture is clear: "Let me in."

Kit's knock meant joining the community at Mount Carmel was something I just had to do. But after returning to Whitehorse, it became clear that I would not be leaving as immediately as I'd thought. Emails from both Kit and Barb revealed that the ongoing internal conflicts at Mount Carmel had thrown the community into even more uncertainty. The next thing I knew, the school year had begun and I was back at work as an Educational Assistant and finishing *Last Stop for Miles* in my spare time.

As time passed, my Mary "yes" had become a Mary "maybe" and, during the months of September and October, *Should I Stay or Should I Go* by The Clash played on mental repeat. Should I stay and continue to live my life in the world, doing my creative work, building my spiritual direction practice and being of service to my student? Or should I go and leave my student and Lukie and the film and my friends and all my support systems? Maybe leaving at Thanksgiving break would be the right thing. Or maybe the Christmas break. Or maybe finish out the school year and just leave in the spring.

In the meantime, and in an attempt to further embrace Catholicism, I attended a couple of Bible Study evenings at the Mary House, home of the Madonna House community. My more-than-literal interpretation of the stories did not necessarily jibe with the very-literal belief system of the group but the MH staff are such loving people that it didn't matter. Just being around them felt good. At the end of one evening, as we chatted informally over tea and listened to the fire pop and crack in their big wood stove, I shared with Ada, one of the staff, my increasing confusion about leaving my established life and the fear of ditching my responsibilities. Ada had been an elementary school teacher and had given up everything in her life to join the MH community. She understood my reticence and told me that she had adored her students and leaving them had broken her heart.

"How did you finally decide?" I wanted to know.

"I realized my home was in the Blessed Sacrament," she told me. "It's not *a* child, Celia. It's *the* child."

She was talking about Jesus. Giving it all up for Jesus. But in my mind, my student was Jesus because she taught me true humility. Day in and day out, my student's vulnerability asked me to look at my own pride, which said, "I am self-sufficient! I can do things by myself!" My student was Jesus because she taught me compassion when she screamed and screamed for no apparent reason. She was Jesus because her suffering shone a light on my own powerlessness and forced me to turn to God for power and inner strength.

At the end of October, I wrote to Kit and Barb and let them know that I needed to finish out the school year. Could I start the following July instead? It wasn't until early December when Kit sent a reply informing me that the community was officially split, her motives for inviting me had not been entirely pure, and more would be known after January. I was irritated, to say the least. She'd been "pulled by God" to invite me! I'd spent four months obsessing about what to do! True to form, I squashed my irritation in favour of being saintly.

> *Mount Carmel's future is very uncertain. What is certain, however, is the call of my heart. And so, there, or here, I must continue to cultivate the contemplative practice that enables me to live from the heart place.*

Winter of 2014 turned to spring. On one hand I knew that I'd found the relationship of a lifetime with my beloved student. Yet, if I stayed with her, I would always wonder if I'd chickened out of leaving everything to go and follow Jesus. Maybe I would eventually start to resent her. With still no word from Mount Carmel, I made a decision to go back to Europe anyway and visit my sister Clara in France and my sister Melissa in

England. If Mount Carmel was still on then I would simply hop over to Ireland. If it wasn't, well, maybe there was somewhere else for me to go. I started looking for places in England, Ireland and France.

For added spiritual sustenance, I'd been attending a Taizé prayer evening, held once a month at the Whitehorse United Church. My first experience with Taizé had been in Vancouver a number of years before. After seeing a poster for an evening of chanting and quiet prayer, I'd attended the service, and enjoyed the brief, emotive songs and silent meditation. When the monthly Taizé prayer began in Whitehorse, initiated by a young woman named Elise, I discovered a worship service that suited me. Scripture was read, not preached, and there was time made for silent meditation. I found the readings from Brother Roger, the founder of the ecumenical Taizé community in France, to be broad-minded and open-spirited, more like calls for transformation than dogmatic lessons.

On one of these Taizé evenings in spring, I told Elise about my search for a community and my upcoming trip to Europe to visit my sisters.

"You're going to be in France?" she exclaimed. "Come to Taizé! I'll be there in July."

Taizé was a community of Brothers, so not a longer-term option for me, but Elise explained that the village of Taizé was also a place for pilgrims to come and spend a week. "It's mostly for young people," she told me, "but older people can come as well." I took her gleeful invitation as a clear nudge from the Universe and went on the Taizé community's website that night. I was indeed "older," as I learned they invite 18-29 year-olds to come and stay to find peace and meaning throughout the year, but adults over 30 are only invited at certain times. July was one of those times, when I would be visiting Clara in Paris.

In late April, still having heard nothing from Mount Carmel, I wrote to Kit and Barb again, telling them I was still committed to coming, believing that despite everything, the knock on the door trumped all. Kit responded a few days later. Her enthusiasm did not match my own.

"Celia, soon we will be having elections. There is no reason to think that the new regime will be interested in our conversation from last summer. I tried to alert you to this possibility in December." She ended by suggesting I write back in a few weeks.

Kit's letter threw me off track. My mind could not figure out what to do and the more I went over it in my head, the less I knew how to proceed. In a state of sleeplessness and unknowing, I returned to the Naramata Centre to attend the first intensive of a second-tier training year with the Pacific Jubilee Program. The nurturing container that is PJP was the best thing for me. With a small group of loving people committed to doing deep soul work on a daily basis, I could share my journey of trying to maintain a peaceful heart in radical uncertainty. All of them offered unconditional support and helpful feedback. Many of them suggested I look for somewhere else to go.

Just found the Faithful Companions of Jesus,
a contemporary congregation of religious Sisters

*in Western Canada who wear their own clothes
and whose members seem younger than most.
But they seem too active. Where, O Lord?*

"Have you looked into the Iona community in Scotland?" one friend asked me during the intensive. I had, actually, but the words "Life here is BUSY" had turned me off. "There is also the Northumbria Community in the north of England," he added. "They're 'new monastics.'"

"Or what about the Taizé community?" offered another. "Taizé has Sisters, you know."

His suggestion held the most promise and a quick search brought me to the Sisters of Saint André, a congregation living in Ameugny, a village adjacent to Taizé, where I would be in July. I immediately wrote and inquired about the possibility of spending some time with their community to discern my vocation.

Halfway through the PJP intensive, during a body prayer session led by Lois, I found myself lethargic and unmotivated to move. Body prayer, a kind of free-form dance, is normally one of my happy places but the cumulative exhaustion of the ongoing mental back-and-forth had finally caught up to me. As the others danced their prayers in the space, all I could do was wrap my arms around one of the large wooden beams holding up the building. I held the wood and it held me. In the embrace, the inner voice spoke:

It doesn't matter where you go. I am here.

Four days later, at the closing party of the PJP intensive, my energy revived by the soul work, I danced my heart out. At the end of the evening, one of the participants who'd been watching me express my bodily joy said, "Are you sure you belong in a monastery, Celia?"

I wasn't sure. That was the problem! I'd received wise pearls such as "you're already a monk" and "it doesn't matter where you go", but the inner niggling, the wondering, the *pull* was not going away.

Back in Whitehorse, I received an email from Barb at Mount Carmel, informing me that the "new regime" had been established. A new prioress would take the leadership reins and she, like Kit, was not confident I'd be accepted. She suggested I contact a contemplative order that had recently built a brand-new home near Whistler, BC. These nuns were Dominicans, an enclosed (cloistered) order of preachers who lived in the Queen of Peace monastery in Squamish. I sent them a heartfelt inquiry, asking if I might come and discern my vocation in their community for an extended period of time. The prioress' response was full of encouragement but ultimately a rejection because of my age. Again ancient at 42, I wrote back to ask why.

"Religious, monastic, Dominican community life forms us," she replied. "The clay of 'one's way of being' is usually well-formed/set by the age of 40. To reshape it at this point could break it … so, why do this when the shape is already wonderful? Formation would become de-formation."

It was true that I was already very well-formed by the world. Was I wasting my time trying to re-form myself?

"Maybe you are exceptionally supple," she suggested, keeping my hope alive. She then suggested I write to the Guest Master to arrange a visit. When I did, I was informed that the service road around the monastery was being torn up and there were no visitors permitted for the next few months.

A few days later, a reply arrived from one of the Sisters of Saint André, the order I'd mistakenly thought were Taizé Sisters:

"It is true that we collaborate with the Brothers of Taizé; however, we are a different order and not their female branch nor a contemplative order and it is important for you to find what can help you to go forward in the way the Lord calls you personally. During your stay in Taizé in July, it will be possible to have a personal conversation with one of our Sisters but there is no possibility to welcome people over 30 years old for a longer period of time in Taizé."

A number of other sites were also recommended by this kind Sister but I felt too numb to investigate. Instead, I sent a letter to Kit and Barb's new prioress at Mount Carmel asking if I could return for a short trial so she could meet me and see if my presence would feel like a good fit for the community. If it did, I assured her, I would commit for a longer stay. She wrote me back immediately to explain that the new direction they were taking at Mount Carmel did not allow a place for me.

I was welcome to "come for a stretch this summer" but there was "no possibility for a longer stay."

Ten months after saying yes to Kit's invitation, I was finally given a solid no. Dympna's words telling me that I was discerning my life, not a place, now felt especially relevant. I'd already bought a plane ticket and sublet my apartment (just in case) to a great guy who would take care of Lukie, and I'd given away most of my stuff. I was going *somewhere*. I just didn't know where.

A few hours after the big no from Mount Carmel, I went for coffee with Sharon, a friend I'd run into back in April when I'd spontaneously attended an Easter Mass at the local Catholic Church. She'd later emailed to suggest we get together, having heard through the grapevine that I was going to live in a monastery in Ireland (small town rumours fly) and wanting to say good-bye. When she got out of her car in the parking lot of the coffee shop, I noticed her surreptitiously tuck a book under her arm. "That's for me," I thought. Inside, after we'd found a table, she pushed the book across the table, smiling.

"I brought this for you," she said. "I pray it everyday." The book was called *Celtic Daily Prayer: Prayers and Readings from the Northumbria Community*.

"Northumbria? Someone *just* told me about the Northumbria Community."

"Maybe you're supposed to go there," she said.

When we were saying good-bye, Sharon plunked a white-beaded rosary in my hand. "Italy," she said, with a wink and a shrug. I thanked her, and promised myself I'd look up how to pray a rosary, never having done so in my life. That night when I turned out the light, those white beads turned phosphorescent green and glowed in the dark. Those crazy Catholics!

The next day, after reading through the Northumbria Community's website, I was struck by their radical approach to "exploring new monasticism." They lived as a "church without walls" and took vows of "availability and vulnerability." A link took me to the site of the Northumbria Community in France, described there as "a House of Christian Retreat and hospitality in Southern Normandy being established for people to come and stay, following a monastic rhythm to the day". The house was called *L'Abri à Suvigny*, the Shelter at Suvigny. I wrote immediately to Jane, the woman who ran the house with her husband, Andrew. She responded the next day, inviting me to stay "perhaps for a month or two initially to see how you find it and where God leads, and then make a decision about whether you want to explore further here or elsewhere as a result of that." At least now I had somewhere to go.

A few days later, I remembered that the Sister of St. André had sent me links and other possible leads to follow. When I re-opened her email, I discovered an attachment from a place called Heaven's House in the UK, run by the Sisters of Contemplation, a Roman Catholic Congregation founded during the French Revolution by a priest called Father Jacques Bienvenu. These Sisters were offering a Spiritual Internship Programme to "women in life transitions or discerning their religious vocation." Breath held, I read on. The two Sisters who ran the community, Sister Bernadette and Sister Martha, required only "a simple commitment to a regular prayer practice and an openness to spiritual and personal growth while living and working" at the House. At the bottom of the flyer was an image of Fra' Angelico's painting of the moment Mary is visited by the angel Gabriel, the moment she says "yes." I could barely stand to hope.

Ten agonizing days later, a reply arrived in my inbox: "The Sisters would like to meet with you and have a chat and see where that discussion might lead. When will you be in the UK?" It was signed, "Hennie."

Through a brief correspondence with Hennie, I discovered she had been doing the Spiritual Internship Programme for over a year and her job was primarily taking care of the office business. Together we established that I'd come to see the Sisters in early July, when I would be in Swindon visiting Melissa.

At the end of June, I jumped in my truck to drive 5,550 km to Port Hope, where I would leave the vehicle at my parents' house and fly to Europe for an adventure that held both promise and uncertainty, taking only what I could carry on my back.

Let go absolutely ...

PILGRIMAGE

e 'how was the monastery', & I say "transformative" or "transformational" & he asks how & I say, "maybe someday I'll tell you," or "it showed me my own poverty," or "it taught u how little I really know about humility, detachment & poverty," "it deepened my faith"; "it centered me more deeply on CHRIST,"; t gave me an understanding of the monastic life, community, mmon life"; "it opened the door for me to continue exploring vocation,". so none of those answers are for him, GOD, ey are all for THEE. BLESS HIM, I CONTINUE TO GIVE HIM TO ou. I CONTINUE TO ASK YOU TO TAKE HIM FROM ME, DID dream about last night? i think i might have //

DID YOU KNOW....

There is no thing more important than this. +

My seven-day drive across the country was well planned. I knew where I would be sleeping every night except one and there were many adventures along the way. Sue, my Madonna House friend, had helped me to arrange a night at the Madonna House field house in Regina, called the Marion Centre, a large, stately building that had once been a printing shop, located in a poor area of town. I arrived in time to go to Mass at the nearby Catholic church and spotted the staff immediately, their thrift-store-chic outfits and crosses giving them away. Still under the impression that it was permissible to take Holy Communion because Kit had said it was okay, I allowed myself to receive the Eucharist.

Back at the Marion Centre, I was made to feel very at home by the staff. The Madonna House charism, or their spiritual orientation and the values to which their order adheres, includes generous hospitality. To the Madonna House staff, a guest is Christ, and they are to welcome and treat guests as such. In the room where I was to sleep, a homemade card made from construction paper and pasted with flowers, lovingly cut from a scrap of wallpaper, said, "Welcome, Celia," in careful calligraphy.

The Marion Centre impressed me. The basement was a thrift store with racks of donated clothes and the first floor housed an industrial kitchen, dining room and recreation area where they served hundreds of meals a day made from donated groceries to the folks living on the margins. But what touched me the most was a comment made by Darlene, who had made me the card, in an intimate conversation after supper. She had been with Madonna House for over fifty years and shared some of her journey. She had known almost nothing about real poverty when she'd arrived, only that she wanted to serve the poor. Doing so for all of these decades had taught her one thing: "I'm the poorest one of all," she confessed.

Darlene was talking about spiritual poverty, a concept I'd been trying to grasp since transcribing all of those passages from *Centered on Christ* at Mount Carmel. She seemed to be saying that the more you have the poorer you are. This idea sat in my heart and burned.

> *I am in this holy place where people live in humble poverty and devote their lives to you and I don't know if I have the courage.*

After a deeply meditative and truly joyful week of driving 10-13 hours a day, I made it to Port Hope to spend some time with my parents. It was hard for them to understand what I was doing. I had found an excellent job in Whitehorse, why was I giving it up? Calling and vocational discernment were unsatisfactory answers, but they listened as I explained and, despite their reservations, said they wanted me to be happy.

Next stop: Paris. I spent some quality time there bonding with my three year-old nephew and helping Clara and her partner pack and prepare for a move back to Canada after 17 years in that fabulous city. Clara was supportive of my journey and, being a comedienne, made fun of me, too. It was good to laugh with her.

Then I headed to Swindon, UK, to visit Melissa and, from there, I would make a day trip to Heaven's House to meet the Sisters of Contemplation. Melissa and I had lived together in Montreal in my early sobriety, and spiritual discussion had been a big part of our relationship. At some point though, God had become a taboo subject with her and I'd stayed away from the topic. Now that we were together again, I asked her why she'd stopped talking to me about spiritual matters.

"You became too evangelical," she said. "It got to the point of being offensive."

She wasn't wrong. I had, at one time, clung to my spiritual awakening and preached as if I'd found the answers to the great mysteries of life, just like I had at age five, when I'd gone to church and then tried to convert the whole family. But time and life lessons had helped me to release some of my fervour and Melissa admitted she now saw a change in me. I owed at least some of this change to a wise elder who had said to me, "You can't be so heavenly that you're no earthly good." His teaching continues to remind me to accept my humanness.

Melissa was not at all supportive of my possible move to a Catholic community. She asked me questions that reflected her own harsh judgments about the Church and triggered a deeper self-doubt in me. Was I again just trying to be heavenly and was I unconsciously seeking spiritual perfection? My journals during those months are filled with prayers for the purity of heart that defines the contemplative monastic.

One afternoon, without telling Melissa, I snuck off to a Catholic Mass. The church was filled with Goans whose colourful clothing brightened the drab interior of the modern brick building. Their faithful worship struck me as something to admire. Yes, the Church is imperfect, I thought, *and* it brings people together.

> *Tomorrow I will go to meet the Sisters. I am excited as can be.*

Hennie picked me up at the train station. She was a lot more hip than I'd expected and she cracked jokes as she drove me through the posh suburb in her retro Nissan Micra. Heaven's House, a former mansion surrounded by other mansions and modest homes, stood quietly amidst the lush gardens I'd seen in the flyer. Hennie told me it was lunch time and took me inside to eat soup with the community.

In the dining room, a simple but grand space with hardwood floors and soaring Victorian ceilings, Sister Bernadette, a tiny Scot in her late 50s, introduced herself, and we made small talk as we waited for Sister Martha and Sylvia, the cook, to come from the conference room across the hall. Sister Martha, a Londoner, was leading a group in a contemplative art class and they were a bit late. She arrived, apologizing for holding us up, and I was struck by her youthful energy. Apparently she was 80-something but looked closer to 60. Sylvia, also Scottish, was fresh-faced and friendly, and she served the soup, which had chicken in it. A vegetarian for fifteen years, I said nothing.

After lunch, Sister Bernadette announced that she and Sister Martha and I would go to the lounge for our meeting. The lounge was another grand room complete with fireplace, giant windows and more of those soaring ceilings. Sister Martha and Sister Bernadette sat together on a loveseat and I took a seat on the end of a long couch.

"So the first thing you need to know, Celia," said Sister Bernadette, "is that we are no longer offering the Spiritual Internship programme."

"Oh," I said, I disguising my shock. "Then what the f*ck am I doing here?" (I didn't say that part.)

The Sisters went on to share how they'd been taken advantage of a number of times by women who'd come for the Internship and then abruptly left the community. They'd felt used and hurt and ultimately decided that the programme didn't really work.

"But then we got your email and we wondered, what is God doing?" said Sister Martha.

"So we knew we had to meet you," finished Sister Bernadette. They asked me to tell them why I thought a Spiritual Internship with them would be a good idea. I relayed the story of my calling and my desire to devote my life to God. When I told them that I could barely stand to hope that this situation would work out, tears came to my eyes and I had to pull myself together. I saw by the kind looks on their faces that they, too, were moved.

"You have so many gifts," said Sister Martha, "we would have to get you doing something very adventuresome. We don't want you cleaning toilets."

"But I'm willing to clean toilets," I said.

We moved on to a tour of the house. Upstairs was a Prayer Room housing the Blessed Sacrament and when we entered, Sister Bernadette bowed and Sister Martha went down to the floor on one knee (known as genuflecting) and I copied her movement. There were a number of large bedrooms for retreatants, another expansive dining room with an adjacent kitchenette, an office where Hennie seemed to spend most of her time and, finally, an art cupboard filled with supplies. When we passed the stairs leading up to the top floor, Sister Bernadette said, "That's private." (I was later to find out it was their apartments.) As we descended the stairs Sister Bernadette said something about my being Catholic.

"I'm not Catholic," I said.

Sister Bernadette stopped and looked back at me. I stopped. Sister Martha, behind me, stopped, too.

"I thought you were."

"I'm not Catholic or Protestant," I said. Sister Bernadette's face changed and Sister Martha jumped in.

"Well, perhaps that will be part of your journey to come," she said and touched my arm.

The Sisters told me they would discuss everything and pray for direction and let me know what they'd decided in a few days. At the door, Sister Martha gave me some pamphlets and said, "Pray for us."

"Really, God?" I said aloud as I walked past the big homes and manicured gardens. It didn't seem like a fit. But going back to Whitehorse didn't really seem possible either. I had left, said good-bye to a way of being.

On the train back to London, reading over one of the pamphlets Sister Martha had given me, I found myself inspired by the story of Father Jacques Bienvenu, the Sisters' founder, and his absolute devotion to contemplation, which he considered to be the cure for the soul-misery of the world, and his passion made me think "maybe Heaven's House" after all.

Next stop: Taizé, in the south of France, to experience the phenomenon of the small order of monastic Brothers who welcome thousands of young people and hundreds of older adults each week. Elise from Whitehorse was there to greet me, thank goodness, because the place is like a bustling hive and I was overwhelmed by the crowds when I arrived.

"Where is your luggage?" she asked me, seeing only my small backpack.

"This is it," I said.

"You'll need a sleeping bag then," she said, and walked me over to El Abiodh, the house for welcoming women pilgrims. The air was hot and dry and young people were everywhere, hanging out, working, congregating in small groups.

"That's the Church of Reconciliation," Elise told me as we passed a massive building, stretching as far as the eye could see. "They have had to keep expanding it for all the pilgrims who come. It can hold about six thousand now."

At El Abiodh, Elise managed to secure me some bedding and I left a note for the Sister with whom I'd corresponded back in May, reminding her that she'd said I could have a personal conversation with one of the Sisters of Saint André during my stay. Elise and I continued walking through the busy village to the bunkhouses, a series of rowed wooden cabins, where I would stay for the next week. I chose a top bunk in a corner and dumped my stuff.

When Brother Roger Schütz founded the community in Taizé, he welcomed men from all different Christian denominations and then wondered how they were going to pray together. "Sing," was the answer they came up with, and then created melodious chants that have now touched countless people all over the world. In my view, this, and the fact that young people are welcomed and encouraged to be themselves, is the key attraction for the thousands. There is no priest at the altar, no one preaching or holding sway over the crowds. There is only song uniting everyone together in literal harmony.

An email arrived from Sister Bernadette inviting me to come to Heaven's House "for a time of discernment from Monday, September 1st, for three months to begin, with a view to continuing till your 6-month UK visa runs out."

Was I glad? Relieved? Excited? I didn't know. But when I went back to one of the booklets Sister Martha had given me, listing the yearly programme for the House (a Centering Prayer retreat, an icon painting course, contemplative art classes, meditation groups), gratitude rushed in and the place seemed much more like a fit.

Journal entries show that I had a lot of anxiety for the first few days in Taizé. Living in a dorm and being surrounded by so many people brought me way outside my comfort zone and I experienced a kind of inner paralysis. I prayed to be of service, which is the quickest way to get myself out of self-centred fear, and was promptly given dish-duty. My prayer was further answered when I was able to connect with a woman named Veerle over the boiling bathtub-sized sink full of plastic plates and bowls. Veerle was really struggling, too, and we exchanged stories about our anxious feelings. She needed to unpack her pain and I told her I was a spiritual director and could listen, if she wished. She did wish and we met later that day on a patch of dry grass in a field under a blue sky. The stark white clouds moved steadily above us and the wind felt like a hot blow-dryer against our skin. Amazingly, Veerle confided a story of childhood sexual abuse. In hearing what she'd had to endure my heart broke open and fear flew away. I was not alone.

Veerle's commitment to overcoming her trauma blew me away. Why are some able to heal and not others? I also felt compassion for her brother, who'd abused her. Over the years, my healing work around forgiving the man who'd molested me, and forgiving my own sexually inappropriate behaviour, had given me the ability to see perpetrators as human beings, not monsters. This is what human beings do. We sexually abuse each other. It's not right but it happens. All the time. We're sick. We need help. And, most of the time, we don't get the help we need. We are all outcasts: victims and perpetrators alike.

Veerle and I talked about this sticky business of shame, forgiveness and acceptance. The sharing we did that day felt like a miracle: Cosmic Knowing bringing us together for more healing to happen.

Each day after breakfast there was bible study. Because breakfast consisted of a bread roll, a piece of chocolate, and a hot drink from a choice of powders, most of us were so hungry we couldn't help but devour the "Word of God." There were about 100 of us "over-thirties," and we'd gather in clusters according to our spoken language to hear the Brother assigned to us take us through the Book of Genesis.

Our teacher, Brother Philipé, was a tall, fit, extremely well-groomed older man with a gentle manner and a good sense of humour. His clothing was immaculate, perfectly ironed, and there was not a hair out of place on his head. He had a cashmere sweater tied around his shoulders and a gold watch on his tanned wrist. He did not look like a poor man. When the study class was over, Brother Philipé got into a big, shiny car and was driven away. A terrible feeling hit my stomach. These Brothers were rich! Was it all a sham? Was this community just another opportunistic cult that took other people's money?

I shared my concern with a Parisian woman in my study group, who scoffed. "Let it go," she said, and told me it was none of my business. Maybe one of the Brothers had been a hairdresser. Maybe Brother Philipé's family sent him cashmere sweaters. Maybe they received that swanky car from a donor and the driver was a willing volunteer. All of her reasoning made sense but I was like a dog with a bone and went to ask one of the Brothers, who make themselves available for questions and support, about their vow of poverty.

"Brother Roger never liked the word poverty," he told me. "He preferred 'material and spiritual sharing.' We don't own our possessions. All the money from the pilgrims goes back into running the village. We sell our wares in the boutique. That's how we make our living."

I know now that being triggered by other people's wealth comes from being ashamed of my own. It's easier to judge others than to feel the shame of my privilege. At the time, I knew enough to keep taking action to shift the judgmental thinking, so I just continued to pray to be of service and keep an open mind about what was being taught to us in the story of Jacob from the Book of Genesis.

> *Jacob left all his securities behind to embark on a long journey. What securities must I leave behind in order to enter into an adventure with God? The desire for security itself.*

Arrangements had been made for me to meet with Sœur Cécile, who had a calm but intense demeanour. We met under a shady tent and the story of my calling unravelled in broken French. Her response was measured and sure and though I failed to understand all she had to tell me, I did hear her unequivocal bottom line: in order to answer the fundamental question of whether I was being called to live my life as a Religious (aka nun) in the Catholic Church, I must undergo the Spiritual Exercises of Saint Ignatius in a 30-day program.

You can imagine what I did next. My internet search for "spiritual exercises of saint ignatius" gave me two hits. One, from a centre in Wales, and one from a centre in Guelph, ON, a couple of hours from Port Hope. Both had retreats at a cost of about $4000 CAD and both were to begin in early January. It was mid-July. There was plenty of time to meditate on the idea.

On one of the last nights, I stayed behind in the church after the prayer to seek further counsel from one of the Brothers. The poverty issue had not gone away, I was navigating the ongoing uncertainty of my future and I just needed guidance, period. As I headed toward the exit, a Black man in priestly robes appearing to be lit from above drew my broken spirit toward him. He graciously agreed to speak with me, introducing himself as Father Pius from Kenya. We sat down together as the dwindling song echoed through the cavernous space.

"I'm struggling with this notion of poverty," I told him. "I come from privilege and yet I'm being eaten by my judgment of the privilege of others. The Brothers look so rich and I can't see their poverty and so I don't trust them."

"You are studying the story of Jacob this week, yes?" asked Father Pius. I nodded. "And Jacob 'grew exceedingly prosperous', yes? You remember? He had many, many servants and came to own large flocks of animals. He had everything, all those camels and donkeys and goats and cows. You remember? Jacob was a rich man! Why? Because he was greedy? No. Because God gave him what he needed to be of service to others." Suddenly I was crying. "Is it okay?" he asked me, looking worried.

"Yes."

"Nothing belongs to us," he continued, softly. "We cannot judge what other people have. We don't know. We are given what we need to serve our brother and sister. Okay? Have I said something for you to understand?"

"Yes, thank you, Father."

We stood and he embraced me and I walked out into the warm night, crickets dominating the quiet, stars blanketing the sky. Reflecting on my journey of discernment, all that had brought me to this place and now looking ahead to the Northumbria Community in France and the Spiritual Internship at Heaven's House brought forth Jacob's response to God for his many blessings:

> *I am unworthy of all the steadfast love and constancy you have shown me.*

ACCEPTANCE

A fter Taizé, I took a train to Vire, where Jane Perkins and her twenty-something daughter, Sarah, picked me up to take me to Suvigny, their Northumbria Community-connected home in Southern Normandy. Jane drove us through the hallowed countryside in her right-steering British car. Here, some of the bloodiest battles of World War II had taken place.

The Suvigny farmhouse had been in a state of disrepair and the surrounding land had been totally barren when Jane and her husband Andrew had bought the property. All had been brought back to life by the work of many hands. They and their fellow British ex-pats had transformed the derelict building into a comfortable dwelling now surrounded by fruit trees and flowering gardens, thick hedges and a living pond with plump white-and-orange koi.

My room on the second floor was actually a single bed surrounded by sheets pinned to a clothesline to make walls. When I Skyped with my parents to let them know I'd arrived safely they said it looked like I was living in a refugee camp. It *was* close quarters but this comparison was far from just. We were all privileged and more than comfortable. The biggest challenge was going to the bathroom, which was just another sheeted area adjacent to the sheeted bedrooms. If you want to learn humility, evacuate your bowels with three pairs of ears listening to you do it.

The Northumbria Community's daily prayer cycle is rooted in Celtic tradition and includes readings and stories from early monks like Saint Patrick and

Saint Columbanus. I'd been faithfully reading and following this cycle in the book Sharon had given me in Whitehorse so I felt at home during the four daily prayer times (morning, noon, evening and night prayer, or Compline, just before bed).

By day four I was ready to leave. Slow down and what happens? The mind ramps up. I was not cut out for community life, my thoughts told me. So I did what I always do when I'm freaking out: I tell on myself. Jane invited me to rest. Not a bad idea since I was starting to get a sore throat. When I came down with a nasty cough it occurred to me that my body might just be totally exhausted after an entire year of stressing myself out in order to do God's will.

After a week of rest, I began to work: trimming the laurel hedges and shovelling stones for a new path and weeding the garden and doing dishes and cooking meals and cleaning toilets and picking fruit to make pies and jam and *clafoutis*. As I worked, the mind went right on trying to figure out the future. Was I being called to become a Catholic nun? The question churned over and around every possible angle. I wanted it. I didn't want it. I wanted it. I didn't want it. I must do it. I can't do it. I must. I can't.

One morning, I went for a meditative run along the country roads, passing fields of goats and cows and horses and smelling the smells that come with them. The sun was high in the sky and the heat was rising from the black asphalt on the road. A breeze cooled the sweat on my skin. It was glorious. But the mental stream of commentary went on and on. As my running shoes padded the pavement a prompt arrived from the inner voice:

> *Quit living the life you think you're supposed*
> *to be living and live the life that you are living*
> *right now.*

I tried. Each day after lunch, during the Quiet Hour, an integral part of the day's rhythm, I'd withdraw to a tiny wooden shed Jane had refashioned as a *poustinia*. My Madonna House friends had introduced me to the Russian word and I knew it to describe a space where one could be alone in the presence of God. Catherine Doherty, the Madonna House foundress, had written a book called *Poustinia* and after Jane had read it she'd felt compelled to transform the ramshackle garden shed into a place to pray, rest, be silent and still. (When I emailed my Madonna House friend Sue to tell her that Doherty had shown up in a remote corner of rural France, she simply replied, "She does that.")

I felt at home in that little shed. The August sun would warm the inside and it smelled and felt like a dry sauna. I'd curl up on the floor and listen to the cows mooing in the nearby fields and the birds chattering in the fruit trees. I would meditate and pray the rosary, finding peace in the uncomplicated rhythm of the Hail Mary, and sometimes I'd fall asleep with the beads between my fingers. If I could manage to stay awake, I'd focus my gaze on an icon of the Madonna and Child, which sat before me on the altar. This particular version of Mary looked like a sexy, Spanish flamenco dancer and her black eyes would draw me in.

"Holy Mary, Mother of God ..."

The constant repetition of the words made me wonder, just who is the *Mother* of God? In the context of the prayer, yes, it's Mary, the mother of Jesus, but I started to think about it from a more cosmic perspective. If God is the Engine that birthed the Cosmos, who birthed the Engine? This question reminded me of my father's conundrum: if there's a God, who made God?

I am created, therefore there is a Creator.

At our meal times, the God subject often came up. One time, Sarah was trying to get her head around the concept of being known personally by God and I was riffing on the idea. "How could an unconscious Universe possibly provide us with consciousness? It only follows that the Cosmos is conscious—" Suddenly, we heard a loud *CRASH* from the kitchen. When we went to investigate, we saw that a glass shelf had seemingly shattered into pieces spontaneously. We could find no obvious reason for the sudden explosion. "You see?" I said to Sarah. "This is nothing less than glass-shelf-shattering God. At the very moment we doubt its existence, it makes itself known to us."

One of Jane's more evangelical friends made a back-handed comment about my views being heretical when I'd made a distinction between the historical Jesus and Christ Energy. While I was disturbed at being called a heretic, I realized that in the eyes of the Catholic Church I was.

But how is it possible to be called by Christ and to be a heretic?

Jane was a great help. Her Christianity was broad. When I told her about my "baptism by desire" in Lake Okanagan, she said, "So you have already been baptized."

"But not according to the Catholic Church. I will still need to be baptized if I decide to become Catholic."

"You can't be baptized twice," she insisted.

"It's not twice if they don't count the first."

Jane had a close relationship with the *Communauté Jerusalem*, a contemporary religious community of Brothers and Sisters who lived in the monastery on the peak of Mont Saint Michel, the famous rock jutting out of the English Channel on the French side. She suggested the Jerusalem community as a possible alternative if my upcoming time with the Sisters of Contemplation did not work out. After researching them online and finding them to be a young and vibrant group of men and women living out their charism "In the City" simply by being with people in the streets, I was intrigued, especially because the founder was a fellow Canadian, from Québec. Jane made an appointment for me with one of the Sisters at the *Mont* and told me she'd take me there herself.

Winding roads, sand-coloured villages and late-summer fields accompanied us to the *Mont* on a sunny afternoon. When it came into view, jutting out of the water just off the coast, I could see the abbey church and its iconic spire at the very top of the rock, reaching up toward heaven as if trying to touch the very hand of God.

To get to the island we had to take a bus over a bridge. People used to walk and drive across the dark sand when the tide was out (apparently some still do) but people kept getting caught by the incoming tide so they built a bridge to save lives (and cars). Time was tight and the bus was very crowded. I was anxious about being late and Jane sensed it. When we got off the bus, I followed close behind her as she legged it up the narrow, crowded streets, up past tourist shops and cafés and bars, up and up and up to the top of the rock where, at the pinnacle, the enormous house built for God sat quietly amidst the countless noisy people who had come to see it.

"There she is," I heard Jane say, indicating a young woman in the simple habit of the *Communauté Jerusalem*: a plain, blue smock and matching headscarf. I had not been expecting Sœur Rose-Marie to be a fresh-faced girl with big, Bambi eyes and lashes to match. She was so young and so pretty I felt like I was meeting the Virgin Mary herself.

Sœur Rose-Marie led me through the crowds, taking a large key out of her apron and opening the abbey gate. Once through, the people disappeared and we walked along a cobblestone lane enclosed by the high walls of the 1000-year-old church on one side and the monastery on the other.

I was ushered through a small, heavy door and we entered a tight hallway, cool and dim. The stone walls were the colour of beach sand and looked newly restored, but the beams across the low ceilings were centuries old. We entered a bright room with a wooden table and two stools and Sœur Rose-Marie began to make us tea. I was drawn to one of the tiny windows that showed how thick the walls of the monastery were, and I bent down to see the view far below us. The tide was out and people, as small as ants, dotted the brown, exposed bottom of the waterway between the *Mont* and the miles of countryside stretching beyond the shore of the mainland.

Over tea and biscuits, I once more told my story in halting French as Sœur Rose-Marie smiled rapturously and listened, her long-lashes batting over her sparkling eyes.

"Do you read the Bible?" she asked me, in French.

I told her that I tried. She said how much reading scripture filled her with happiness. She was so full of joy that I almost didn't believe her. How did this ravishingly beautiful young woman with the flawless skin, perfect teeth and lips of a movie star end up a nun before the age of 30? It was simple: her love of God and her desire to serve. She had actually converted to Catholicism in order to join the Jerusalem Community.

Sœur Rose-Marie then told me about a program offered by her order called *Un An Pour Dieu* (a year for God), and suggested that I look into their community in Montreal. I assured her that I would. (And did. Their monastery turned out to be kitty-corner to the National Theatre School, where I'd gone to school for two years.)

Back at Suvigny, I was hit by a wave of despair. How could I become a monk when I didn't believe that the Bible was the literal word of God? That night, I went for a walk in the dark. Two-hundred and fifty billion mysteries twinkled above me. It was so quiet I could hear a herd of cows huffing and puffing in the field next to the road. Their breath brought me back to the here and now. "Quit living the life you think you're supposed to be living and live the life that you are living right now, Celia," I whispered, reminding myself.

Jane knew I was interested in the Little Flower (Saint Thérèse of Lisieux) and the Carmelite order she had joined at the age of 15, and she gave me a DVD of a documentary called *No Greater Love*.

"It's about a Carmelite convent in Notting Hill, London," Jane said, "Apparently the filmmaker spent six years persuading the nuns to let him film their lives. It's very good."

I watched the DVD with fascination, feeling like Thérèse had personally arranged the viewing from her heavenly perch, fulfilling her dying vow to spend her time in heaven "doing good on earth." The Little Flower's presence turned out to be one of the beating hearts of the Monastery of the Most Holy Trinity, the nuns' home. Here was a community of women living out the extraordinarily difficult charism of the Carmelite order, one that keeps them separated from the outside world, enclosed in full habits and cloistered rooms to avoid distraction, toiling away at manual tasks and praying for hours and hours a day. A scene showing four of the nuns folk-dancing together revealed how much intimacy and fun could be found in a simple, shared dance and how their joy came from being together, when they were allowed.

What affected me the most was the Carmelite notion of total self-gift: giving all for God. Again, I told myself that this was the only way to live. Every other path led to a pseudo-life. And yet, because my personal path to God had taken so many other paths, the Way of Carmel also seemed so limited. But not wanting to leave any stones unturned, I wrote a letter to the prioress of The Monastery of the Most Holy Trinity, sharing with her my love of the film, my desire for God and my curiosity about the Carmelite vocation.

My emotions continued to waver. I was having dreams about defecating in public, evidence of how vulnerable I was feeling. Mind you, I *was* defecating in public, in the bathroom with sheets for walls. Yard work kept my mind off the future. Walks in the country kept me sane. One afternoon, I walked for two hours to Mortain, a medieval village. On the way, I came across a dead tabby tomcat on the side of the road, his back-legs splayed open exposing his big, furry balls. His head was bashed in and I alternated between staring down at him in horror and looking around for someone to tell. Eventually, I rolled him as gently as I could into the ditch with my foot to give him a more dignified resting place. Somewhere in me there were tears for him, and I stayed with his little body for a while, trying to summon them. They wouldn't come.

At a busy roundabout, a giant cross had been mounted on a platform on the side of the road. It was the exact same version as the cross in the cemetery at the foot of the Bull Mountain, with two stone figures at its base, looking up woefully at the crucified Jesus. (Is there a commercial mold for these things?) It began to lash with rain but I went to kneel at its foot to pray. The water poured down my back and soaked my clothes as the cars zoomed by.

> *I'm at the foot of the cross. I'm praying to the symbol of Christ and I'm thinking about what the people going by in their cars will think of me. This is the root of my problem.*

On August 25th, my time in France came to an end. With nowhere to go for the five-day gap between Suvigny and Heaven's House, I'd arranged to stay at a Madonna House field house in Robin Hood's Bay, North Yorkshire. I was grateful for the chance to transition with another branch of this loving community before heading south to live with the Sisters.

Jane and Sarah were heading back to the UK for Sarah's return to University via a drive to Le Havre and a ferry to Portsmouth and I hitched a ride with them. Jane suggested we make a stop in Lisieux to visit the relics of Saint Thérèse and we headed to Carmel de Lisieux, the convent Thérèse had entered at fifteen by special permission from the Pope because she was too young to officially join.

We ate lunch beside a statue of Thérèse that didn't look like her photos, which show a broad-faced young woman with handsome features. Her statue was a slimmed-down, prettied-up, delicate lady. Inside the convent I discovered similar models. The realistic-looking Thérèse lying in her tomb behind a glass case is a more feminine version of the woman in the historical photos. This irritated me. I sat in front of her glass tomb and tried to speak to her, to share what was in my heart. But this just brought more agitation and discontent.

Our next stop was a Basilica that had been built in Thérèse's honour. I was shocked to see that such an enormous beast of a building had been erected for a woman who was known for her Little Way. She had given up everything for her Lord and it was like the Church was trying to give it all back and then some. Thérèse had suffered in illness, strived for perfection in humility, come to know her poverty as a virtue and her individuality as absolutely irrelevant. This is what was being venerated, her absolute, supreme devotion. But it felt wrong, somehow, to worship her with such grandeur. I was offended on the Little Flower's behalf. "This is how much you are loved," I thought, "and it is the complete reverse of who you are."

Feeling sick about the Church and my judgement toward it, I sought Jane's counsel on the drive to the ferry. Just telling her how I was feeling instantly relieved the mounting gloom and helped me to see an old pattern: when I feel like no one is getting it right it's usually because I feel like *I'm* not getting it right. Perfectionism had once again stealthily crept in, accompanied, no doubt, by the low-level anxiety traceable to all the unknowns lying ahead of me.

> *I am slowly giving up on the calling. I am set so firmly in the world. I cannot find my way back to the reverence I had last summer. I've lost my faith. I've given up, in a way, on the church.*

REJECTION

DO THOU TO OBEY ...

THY ASSISTANCE. PLEASE GOD.
dec 27 924p   ST JOHN

IN PRAYER
ONCE MORE
I DECIDED
OR
IT CAME
TO ME
TO LET GO
OF HOLD-
ING
BACK
FOR
IT

IS NOT
BRINGING
ME
ANYTHING
BUT
GRIEF
AND
MISERY
SO
ONCE
MORE
I
LET
GO

150

T he bus to Yorkshire took ten long hours but I was happy to have uninterrupted time to pray and meditate and be alone. Red and yellow-brick towns gave way to purple untamed moors and distant glimpses of the grey North Sea. As we approached Robin Hood's Bay, I could see the high cliffs named for the man of the famous legend.

Diane, the Robin Hood's Bay house director, was waiting for me at the bus station, wearing the familiar cross of the Madonna House apostolate around her neck. We hugged as if we were old friends and then she veered around the twists and turns of the steep roads leading down to the Robin Hood's Bay house, an old country manor surrounded by private gardens and farmer's fields that had been donated to the Madonna House organization. Upon entering the house, I was struck by the fact that yet another once-regal house with high-ceilinged rooms decorated with fancy trim and crown moldings was now inhabited by voluntary beggars devoted to serving those in need of hospitality.

The small community consisted of one man and two other women. Coincidentally, I knew one of the women from when she'd been assigned to the Mary House in Whitehorse. She and I embraced and marvelled at the fact that we were meeting again in this faraway place.

After a simple supper, Diane showed me to the bedroom where I would sleep. It doubled as the library, with a single bed and sink tucked behind bookshelves lined with volumes of spiritual reading.

"We go to Mass at 9 o'clock," Diane told me as she bid me good-night, "But you're welcome to sleep in."

"Oh, I'm coming to Mass," I said. Her eyes widened and she smiled.

"Good," she said, and closed the door.

I found an old newsletter to read containing an article about Catherine Doherty, the Madonna House foundress, affectionately known as "B" or "the B", for "the Baroness", Doherty's title in Russia before she emigrated to Canada in 1921. B had been a lover of God and a faithful servant, renouncing personal wealth and inspiring her community to do the same. She was married and loved her husband devotedly but realized she couldn't well ask the Madonna House apostolates to promise celibacy if she wasn't celibate herself. So she and her husband started to live apart while living together in the same community. This decision broke both of their hearts, but they stuck to it anyway.

B had been baptized Eastern Orthodox but later became a Roman Catholic and the article talked about her spirituality and her religion, as if they were two intrinsically connected yet separate aspects of her being. It occurred to me that I might have found a loophole. Maybe I could become a Catholic but still hold on to my own individual spirituality! The next morning, on the way to Mass, I mentioned this to the lone man in the community. "I think I may have found a Divine Loophole," I told him, but he laughed in a way that told me I hadn't.

The priest saying Mass that morning was an irreverent, jovial Irishman named Father Cian. I stuck out like a sore thumb in the little village church with my shaved head and my miniskirt-and-leggings and he went out of his way to single me out. "We have someone new here today," he said. "Who are you?" Before I could say anything, Diane introduced me, explaining that I was staying with them. "You're very welcome!" boomed Father Cian, in the Irish way. When it came time for Holy Communion, I went up and received the Eucharist like everybody else. The permission I'd been given by Kit, the monk from Mount Carmel, still held sway, in my mind anyway.

That afternoon, Diane and I met in the garden to talk about my vocation. It was sunny and hot and we were surrounded by flowers and gnarly bushes hiding chattering birds. I told her about my baptism by desire, my draw to Catholicism and my current reservations.

"I'm a convert," she told me, and then shared that it had not been easy for her to convert to Catholicism because her family was very much against it, but she had known deep down that it was the only path for her.

"Maybe I can keep it a secret from my family," I said. We laughed, but I was only half-joking.

"Dive deep," she said. "You will know. The Good Shepherd will lead you."

"I don't understand it," I said, suddenly getting choked up, "but it's who I am. It consecrates everything."

"That is what you can say when you feel the need to explain why you want to be baptized. Just that. That is your truth."

I nodded and wiped my tears. Then Diane said she'd noticed that I'd received Holy Communion that morning. "I didn't want to say anything and it's not for me to judge, but technically it is illegal for you to be receiving the Eucharist as a non-Catholic." I felt a jolt of shame at hearing the word "illegal." It made it sound like a crime, and somewhere inside of me, a little girl felt very afraid.

"But I was given permission by a monk. A nun. I thought it was okay."

Diane shook her head. "She had no ecclesial authority to do that." I told her I hadn't known that. "God gave you an amazing gift with your baptism by desire but … no, it's not right."

Humiliation seeped in. I'd been doing something wrong, something illegal, and therefore I was bad. Without knowing it, I internalized the shame. One thing I did know was that diving deep could only happen in solitude. "I need to make a *poustinia*," I told Diane.

Armed with my journal and a pen and some bread and peanut butter, I headed across the garden to the shack built entirely from begged materials by the staff's loving hands. Inside was a bed made from old doors and a table fashioned from used plywood. A very large Bible sat below a print of a fading icon of Jesus. Recycled Georgian windows looked out onto a recently-cut hayfield sloping upward to a grove of trees. Everything had been made from discarded and scavenged materials and yet the little room felt like a palace of peace.

Determined to overcome my resistance to becoming a Catholic, to let go of my pride and my fear of being misunderstood and judged by my family and others, I decided to try and "enter" the Bible and see what happened. I knew *The Gospel According to Saint John* was possibly the most evangelical of the four Gospels. Maybe if I went through it chapter and verse, highlighting the word "believe," it would help me to address my own disbelief. Maybe then I could submit. By the end of the fourth chapter, the struggle had not abated. In some instances it had grown stronger.

> *If I simply "believe" then I'm a fool. Could you be a fool for God? Yes. I love God more than anything else in the world.*

But I kept getting stuck whenever I thought of the exclusive rules of the Roman Catholic Church. They were contrary to what I experienced God to be. Jesus was a man of inclusivity, a man who welcomed everyone to the table no matter what. How could I convert to a religion that made Jesus Lord but denied his basic teachings? Because God was asking me to? What evidence did I have to back this notion up? I had Kit's knock on the door and the call of my heart. Okay, then all I had to do was rid myself of the dualistic blocks of scepticism and righteous condemnation. No biggie.

That night, I fell asleep early and was wakened in the middle of the night by what felt like a Great Presence in the room. With eyes open and breathing slowly, I lay still, experiencing a heightened energy that gripped my whole body. "Is that you, Lord?" I finally asked. Aware of the Jesus icon across the room, I said, "I want to see your face." Next to the bed was a candle and I struck a match and lit the wick. The light from the flame reflected on the print and the face of Jesus disappeared.

So did the feeling of Great Presence. "When you try to see it, it vanishes," I said aloud to the quiet.

My bladder was full and I went outside into the black night to use the compost toilet. There were no stars. Only the sound of crickets. I could see nothing and felt my way around like a blind woman.

When I got back into bed, sleep would not come. My thoughts ran wild with the conviction that the Great Presence in the room had actually been Father Jacques Bienvenu, the founder of the Sisters of Contemplation, calling me to become a nun in their congregation. Being convinced, it followed that I must go to Mass in the morning and ask Father Cian to baptize me.

Morning light finally appeared. Mist rose from the fields outside the window. Was the acute mental clarity I'd experienced in the middle of the night some kind of mania? "Thy will, not mine be done," I whispered to the breaking day.

It was still a good few hours before Mass. As the morning wore on, I became more and more certain that I was to be baptized that morning and more and more nervous about it. I decided to write a letter to God to work through my churning emotions.

> *You make all things possible. What are you going to do with me?*

As I was getting ready to leave the *poustinia*, I heard a thunderous noise outside and looked out the window. Two stags were running at full speed down the field toward the shack. They ran together, as though they were fused at the chest, like a two-headed animal with one body, leaping over the fence beside the shack and disappearing from my sight, the pounding of their hooves fading as they headed into the forest beyond the garden.

"It was like they were saying, 'Go and do it! Go and do it now!'" I said to Diane on the way to Mass, having told her everything, including my vision of Father Jacques. She was dubious.

"It's rare that a priest would just baptize a person on the spot. There are certain protocols to be followed. But Father Cian is the kind of priest that just might do it."

When we got to the church we sat in the parking lot for a few moments before going in. Diane said a prayer, then, "God is in charge. Let's see what happens."

We sat in the pews waiting for Father Cian to come down the aisle. The doors opened behind us and the procession approached: first the Bible, held up by a parishioner, then the Cross, held up by another, then the choir, then the priest. As he passed, I turned to look. It was not Father Cian, the liberal priest who might break the rules and baptize me with no questions asked. It was a visiting priest, who would not.

When it came time to receive the Eucharist I went up with everyone else, only this time Diane's words had taken hold of me. "It's illegal." I knew the drill from my days at the Anglican church in Port Hope and crossed my arms over my chest to receive a blessing instead of Holy Communion. As I walked back to my seat the choir began to sing *Amazing Grace*. Sliding into the pew beside Diane, I put my hands over my face and wept.

PART THREE
GIVING UP

BEGINNING

On the long bus ride back to London from North Yorkshire, I again had time to meditate, reflect and pray. A recent conversation with one of my sober friends back home had brought forth the question *What do you want?* and I was wrestling with it. Partially because I just *didn't know* but mostly because I'd read somewhere that you can't have anything you *want* (i.e. lack) so asking me "what do you want" was like asking me "what do you wish *not* to have?" Yet again, I was overthinking it, trying to get it right. Nevertheless, by re-wording the question to "what do you desire?" the answer came:

I desire to live a holy life.

It seemed so simple. There was no attachment, no expectation, no demand. After the turmoil of the Madonna House experience, this little truth restored me to peace and I walked from the train station to Heaven's House with a sense of excitement and a rock song in my heart.

I rang the doorbell and waited. And waited. My stomach dropped. Had I come at a bad time? Right in the middle of prayers or supper? Finally, Sister Bernadette answered the door.

"Welcome, Celia," she said. "We've just begun Evening Prayer so I think it's best to show you to your room and you can relax there until supper time." I apologized and she waved it off, ushering me into the Ivy Room, where I would be staying for the duration of the Spiritual Internship.

The high ceilings made the room feel much bigger than it was. It was nicely decorated but sparsely furnished with a single bed, wardrobe, desk and chair. Two towering windows on either side of the room gave the room its light: one had frosted-glass to hide the parking lot of the neighbouring school and one had a view of the garden on the north side of the house. A door led to a kitchenette I would be sharing with Hennie, whose room was next door, and another to the back garden. When I opened the back door to go out, spiders tumbled down from the grooves. Stepping into the garden brought me face-to-face with a diminutive statue of Father Jacques. "Did you bring me here?" I asked him. He said nothing, holding his cross close to his chest.

The daily rhythm of the community included daily Mass and saying the Divine Office in the morning, at noon and before dinner. In those first few days, it felt as though I had finally landed in a safe harbour. The last year and all of its where-to-go turmoil and subsequent inner storm of confusion was lifted from me. I was *here*, in a place where my spiritual life could be supported. My journal entries reflect my excitement and gratitude for this reprieve:

> *Lord, I do not know if I am in fantasy land but I am experiencing a vision of becoming a Sister of Contemplation. To have found a home, to have searched & followed & listened & waited & wondered & hoped & died & cried & grieved & trusted & loved & surrendered, O thanks God!*

Within a week of my being in the community, the Sisters invited me up to their private apartments to have a chat. A funny feeling passed through me as I walked up the grand staircase to the upper rooms. I felt important, as though I was being included in something I'd been previously denied.

The three of us sat in the Sisters' lounge, a great room decorated in warm pastel colours and cozy furniture. The tips of sails could be seen moving back and forth across some unseen water in the distance, and the early-September sun gleamed on the glass coffee table between us. I sat on an overstuffed white couch practically swinging my legs like an excited child. The Sisters wanted to know how I was doing, how it had been going for me since I'd arrived. They'd left me pretty much to myself and they apologized for not being more attentive.

"Maybe it's only a pink cloud," I said, after telling them of my growing happiness, "but I'm enjoying it while it lasts."

"We're glad you're here, too," Sister Bernadette said. "It's amazing how good of a fit it is."

"Like a glove," said Sister Martha.

I spoke about the unshakeable feeling that Father Jacques had drawn me to the community and how attracted I was to his vision of contemplation as a "cure for the soul-misery of the world." We talked about how my skills as a spiritual director and facilitator could flourish in the House. Both Sister Bernadette and Sister Martha agreed that exciting possibilities lay ahead. I saw so much potential, I told them, and threw out ideas such as providing contemplative retreats for more marginalized people, not just the privileged who could afford the luxury.

"I've done service work with women in jail and worked with people with special needs. There's a refugee crisis in Europe right now. There's so much to offer here!" The Sisters listened attentively. "I'm also feeling bad about taking up the Ivy Room. Hennie and I occupy the only two accessible guest rooms in the house. What if someone in a wheelchair wants a retreat? Or a person who can't handle the stairs? There's no way to accommodate them right now." This prompted a brief conversation about the possibility of some kind of indoor elevator and I promised to do research to find out about options. "Could we also talk at some point about the process of becoming a novice?" I asked them. "I'm curious to know what that would look like."

"Of course," said Sister Bernadette, "But you can only discern one thing at a time. First you must discern whether becoming a Catholic is right for you."

"I did find a weekly course on Catholicism in London," I told them, "May I go?" They were happy for me to sign up and encouraged me to participate. Sister Martha would offer me spiritual direction once a week, and I could continue to help out in the House with the cleaning and organizing and general run of the maintenance of things for now. Bigger projects would come later.

When I met Hennie in the hallway I told her about my conversation with the Sisters and my desire to possibly join their congregation as a novice.

"Already?" she asked, skeptically. Her reticence stopped me in my tracks. It *was* pretty fast. Like a whirlwind romance or falling in love before you really get to know the person. I had to admit it was the same thrilling feeling as the honeymoon period in relationships, when the red flags of reality are temporarily hidden.

When I found myself in a charity shop at the end of the road trying on navy blue skirts and twirling around in the mirror to see how they fit, it occurred to me that I might be insane. Sister Martha had already told me the story of a woman who had wanted to become a nun simply so she could wear the habit. Recalling the feeling of importance I'd felt going up to the Sisters' apartments, I wondered how much of my attraction to religious life was being motivated by that childlike desire to belong, which can often carry on into adulthood.

What brought certainty about becoming a Religious (a person living in vowed orders) was the feeling I got from attending Daily Mass. I absolutely loved it. Catholics are obliged to go to Mass on Sundays and missing it is considered a mortal sin by the Roman Catholic Church. Daily Mass is a choice for laypeople, and a built-in component of life for Religious. From Monday to Friday, I'd walk across the road in silence with Hennie and the Sisters to a chapel that had originally been built by their order. The adjoining building, once their convent, now belonged to a community of priests, and a handful of them would take turns saying the Mass each morning. Each priest had a different style. One would take his time, performing the ritual with great deliberation. Another one always seemed like he had a train to catch. Father Eamon, their director, would often sit with us in silence rather than give a homily.

It didn't matter to me who said the Mass. I had to cross my arms each morning to receive a blessing rather than the Eucharist, but I still looked forward to this quiet, prayerful and private time shared with only a handful of people from the neighbourhood. In the silence before and after, I would kneel on the kneeler-bar, hands folded, and repeat a sacred phrase silently, sometimes watching the light move across the altar, often meditating on the suffering Jesus, whose bleeding body was suspended from the ceiling on a cross. If my mind was in obsession, which it often was, I would quietly beg for mercy. A couple of times, I was overcome by emotion and wept, unexpectedly. The depth of my grief continued to confound me but when I remembered that "crying is healing," I chalked it up to that.

One particularly memorable emotional deluge arrived after a private mass with a priest-friend of Hennie's who had come to Heaven's House for a visit. Hennie had known Father Peter for many years before he moved to Egypt, where he now lived and served, and he was making a special trip to see her while back in the UK. The Sisters were away and so it would just be the three of us having lunch and Mass together. To have a priest come for an afternoon is not just an opportunity for a visit, it is an opportunity to receive the Eucharist, which, for Catholics, is everything.

"Do you like living in Egypt?" I asked Father Peter over lunch in the dining room.

"I like it wherever I am," he said.

I asked him about the idea of "call" and he described his own calling as a nagging, irritating feeling that would not let go until he attended to it. "My formation has continued to evolve even after I said yes to the priesthood," he told us.

I decided to bring up the Big Three and told him about the chasm between my own intrinsic values and the Catholic teaching on abortion, homosexuality and the ordination of women. Father Peter addressed each of my points carefully and with great kindness but essentially deferred to the doctrinal teachings of the Church: women should have the child even if they couldn't look after it; homosexuals were loved by God but still committing sin; Jesus gave only his twelve apostles permission to consecrate his body and blood and therefore no woman could ever perform the ritual.

"Has this been helpful?" he asked me. I nodded, meekly, wanting to please him and not wanting to argue or show my misery and hopelessness. Again: how could I ever become a Catholic? Earlier in the week, I'd heard another priest say that love was more powerful than doctrinal truth and I clung to those hopeful words as we cleared the table and did the dishes. But I'd been triggered by Father Peter's bias and my mood was darkening. The negative judgment toward the Church continued to chew a hole inside of me as I climbed the stairs to the Prayer Room, dreading the refusal and the rejection that would come when I had to cross my arms and receive a blessing from Father Peter instead of Holy Communion.

A makeshift altar had been set up and Hennie and I sat in front of it while Father Peter said the Mass. Light streamed in through the great windows. There was an intense level of intimacy with just the three of us in the quiet space, accompanied only by a sun-faded icon of Jesus, a small, primitive wood-carved crucifix, and the Blessed Sacrament housed in a simple wooden box.

"What brings you contentment?" Father Peter asked during his homily, looking into my eyes. "Is God enough for your happiness?" He was doing a good job of acting as if he was speaking to a room full of faithful parishioners while subtly directing his questions at me alone. "Like the deer that yearns for running streams, so my soul is yearning for you, my God," Father Peter read.

This is when the flood of tears rushed in. At the mention of the deer, the animal that had appeared at such significant moments in my life, a sensation of being loved and being known returned. But then it felt even more cruel to be refused Holy Communion when I had been so intimately included in the Mass and so cosmically touched.

Was God enough for my happiness? My immediate response was yes, of course, because I wanted to be good. I wanted to be the good, surrendered nun who is God's beloved alone. Ever-determined, I filled out an application to St. Beuno's, the Jesuit centre in Wales, to undergo the Spiritual Exercises of Saint Ignatius as per Sœur Cécile's instructions in Taizé. She had told me this was a necessary step in answering the fundamental question of whether I was being called to become a Religious. It was costly but I had saved a lot of money while working as an Educational Assistant in Whitehorse and could afford it.

"Are you committed to knowing the Lord through the Gospel?" asked the application. The question stopped me cold. Was I? Trusting that the process would allow me to work creatively or figuratively around the question rather than having to answer it literally, I wrote "yes."

"What is your religious denomination?" Yikes. "Currently discerning," was my honest reply. In a descriptive paragraph about the mystical baptism in Lake Okanagan, I attempted to further explain my unorthodox religiosity: "By Grace, I have been given the gift of faith," I wrote, "I did not create this passion for God. It has been given to me." This was also my way of reassuring myself.

What appeared before my eyes when I was at my lowest? The cross. When I was at my most terrified, what had I seen? The face of Jesus.

Had I created these encounters? Maybe. But they had also confirmed, for me, that the Great Reality, in which we are all immersed, knew me and made Itself known to me, and I was committed to living from that knowing.

This experiential reality, this awareness of Higher Guidance, ran as a supportive undercurrent to the "to-convert-or-not-to-convert" question, as did my connection to the natural world. A flock of bright-green, wild parakeets would greet me each morning on the way to Mass, dive-bombing in the air above the front garden. They made me laugh and filled me with wonder. Where had they come from? The flow of the nearby River Mole and the swans and ducks paddling on its surface never failed to calm my anxiety. The parkland that surrounded the river had open fields lined with great trees and patches of forest containing secret pathways wild with tangles of bramble and bracken. I'd walk in these spaces and find solace and joy. I also made the happy discovery of the reservoir where I'd seen the tips of sailboats moving back and forth from the Sisters' lounge. One day, I even snuck through the gate to watch the boats close up. Then, around the other side of the reservoir, I found a flock of sheep feeding on the steep, grassy sides. Watching them contentedly munch the grass while their lambs gambolled and baa-ed made everything okay.

> *I cannot figure this thing out. I just have to keep showing up.*

I'd told the Sisters that I'd found an indoor home elevator online that was relatively simple to install and seemed to require minimal disruption. They said it sounded interesting and I took that to mean we would go ahead, so I began clearing out two large closets, one on the ground floor, and the other directly overhead on the floor above, the perfect corresponding locations. I threw away the obvious junk but organized the keeper items by lining them up in the hallway for review by the

Sisters. When I showed them what I had done, Sister Martha was not pleased.

"But what can you have been thinking?" she asked me, unable to hide her displeasure.

"I thought we'd talked about an elevator to make the House more accessible—"

"No, no, no," she said, "There's not going to be any elevator."

"It's alright," said Sister Bernadette, trying to defuse the situation, "It's a good idea, Celia, maybe just not right now."

Feeling more than a little ashamed, I replaced the boxes and items of small furniture and did not mention it again. But it did not take long for my mind to shift to the next project: to make the Ivy Room available to someone who might really need it. After all, I could climb stairs. Maybe I could even live in the attic! Clean it out and put a little mattress and table up there. Then all of the handicapped people who were flocking to Heaven's House could have this wheelchair-accessible room that I was taking away from them.

"You wouldn't last a week in the attic," said Sister Martha after I told her my plan. "What is this about, Celia?"

"I'm just so privileged," I said, referring to the fact that I'd never really wanted for anything. "My family is white, upper-middle-class and educated and in order to really and truly be a 'poor monk' I need to strip myself of it—"

"It's not your job to strip yourself of anything. That is God's job. God is the one who does that for us."

"But I've been given so much. I want to give it all back—"

"You'll never be able to," she said.

This struck me very hard. Maybe this was my poverty. I could never return to God the gifts I'd been given. How could I give back my very existence to Existence Itself?

"Sometimes I think my only motivation to become a Catholic is so that I can become a saint. Other times I think it's because I want to change the Church and if I convert then I can do it from the inside. I could be part of a new reformation movement. Become the first female priest. But then I'd probably be killed."

Sister Martha just looked at me. I knew I was being dramatic. She changed tactics. "It might surprise you to hear me say this but God is not the Church."

"But I have to join the Church to become a nun. And how am I supposed to convert with all of these reservations?"

"Oh, don't worry about it!" she exclaimed. "God doesn't care whether you are a Catholic. God is living inside of you," she said, putting her hand to her heart, "So it doesn't matter whether you are Catholic or Protestant or choose this one or that one. All of this thinking about it is simply a distraction. You have been brought here for a purpose and it has something to do with the contemplative element so ... just do your spiritual reading and try to spend an hour a day in quiet prayer."

So far I was proving to be a pretty lousy contemplative. Despite the hours of quiet prayer and meditation there were distractions. I spent a ridiculous amount of time researching whether it was economically viable to pay off my cell phone contract in Canada and get a new UK number and account. I was online every evening with a dizzying array of people back home: the Pacific Jubilee folks for the second-tier training program I'd begun, spiritual direction clients I'd continued to accompany, and sober friends I was helping and who were helping me. Sister Martha had noticed.

"But *every night*, Celia?" she'd asked me during another exchange.

"These are my lifelines," I'd told her. This was true. And yet I knew she was partially right: I was playing with distraction. Not to mention my efforts at trying to finish *Last Stop for Miles*. A legitimate project, but still. At least I'd told Sister Bernadette how the film's completion was hanging over me and consulted with her about what to do.

"You've made a commitment," she said. "You'll feel better about yourself if you keep it."

"It's a pretty heavy story," I explained, "there are a couple of steamy sex scenes and a stabbing scene and a lot of swearing. Do you think the film will have any negative impact on my becoming a nun if I decide to follow that path?" She didn't seem to think so.

In a long-distance call with one of my Pacific Jubilee mentors, I talked over my discernment process and how I felt like I was pretty much failing in the spiritual life. "I'm hardly an interior person because I don't really give God full measure," I told her. This woman knew me well and had witnessed some of my extreme patterns in the past. She helped me to see that I'd unwittingly allowed the Merciless Taskmaster to get back in the driver's seat. Rigid perfectionism was once again trying to get the spiritual life "right" so I could succeed at my vocation. "Maybe my vocation is actually to fail," I said, after agreeing with her. "That way every time I fail I'll be succeeding in my vocation."

"Dearheart," she said, "That is perfect."

CHURCH-HOPPING

"W hat time will we be going to Mass in the morning?" I asked the Sisters one Saturday evening after supper.

"We won't be going to Mass in the morning," said Sister Bernadette, "We've already fulfilled our obligation by going this evening."

I didn't understand. Hennie explained to me that attending Mass on Saturday evening counted as going to Sunday Mass. The Church had extended the opportunity to Catholics in order to accommodate people in the modern world whose jobs prevented them from getting to Sunday Mass.

"Only you're not meant to use it to have a lie-in on Sunday morning," she said, "But people do."

Going to church for me had never included the pressure to fulfil an obligation. I'd started going because I wanted to sing and I'd kept on going because I loved the ritual, the opportunity to say thank you and to offer my reverence for the Great Mystery of Life. Yes, I'd just been to Mass that evening *and* I felt like going again in the morning. So, partly out of a sense of rebellion and partly because I was craving familiarity, I searched "protestant church near me" and discovered St. Paul's Anglican nearby. Their webpage had a rainbow banner and the words: "We are an inclusive Church. Here everyone is welcome and everyone belongs."

The next morning, I walked the short distance to the church, a late-19th century classical structure complete with a stone tower and spire. Upon arriving at the door, a finely-dressed woman took my hand and warmly welcomed me, asking me where I'd come from and introducing me to others so I wouldn't feel alone. In the Catholic church, you're lucky if anyone even looks you in the eye! Not because they're unfriendly but because the time before the Mass is not for socializing, it's for sitting in reverence in the presence of the Blessed Sacrament. The silence and private worship is my preference but being acknowledged that morning meant a lot.

The minister, Reverend Matthew, was an affable man in his fifties and his sermon was intelligent and compassionate. When it came time for Holy Communion I wasn't sure what to do so I crossed my arms over my chest to request a blessing. Reverend Matthew's face changed and I could tell he was wondering about my gesture as he blessed me.

After the service, I was invited to stay for tea and Reverend Matthew came over to speak with me. Within minutes, I had told him I was living at Heaven's House and struggling with a call to convert to Catholicism. Without being pushy, he made a case for the Anglican Church, explaining how it had all the depth of the Catholic Mass but with a fully inclusive stance. He didn't ask why I'd crossed my arms instead of receiving the Eucharist but I was curious to hear what he would have to say about it.

"I asked for a blessing because I've been told it's illegal in the Catholic Church," I explained, "and I just wasn't sure what was allowed here."

"First of all, we would never use the term 'illegal,'" he said. "You are more than welcome to receive the Eucharist here." His utter acceptance and generous invitation brought a lump to my throat. No prerequisites. He touched my arm and said, "We would love to have you come back."

Later that afternoon, I shared my experience with Hennie. She validated my desire to belong to a church with inclusive values but, in her mind, no Protestant faith could ever offer what Catholicism could.

"Don't you desire the *full* communion experience?" she asked me.

"Of course I do," I said.

"In the Catholic Church you're receiving something that has been consecrated by a priest who has been ordained in a direct, unbroken lineage for the last 2000 years, right from Jesus to Saint Peter and all the way down to Pope Francis. It's the full-meal deal."

Hennie's claim brought up conflicting emotions. On one hand, I felt like I was missing out on something really important. On the other hand, I had already come to know full communion with God through countless mystical experiences. It seemed to me that all this power given to the priest overshadowed the true power of God to work through *everybody and all things*. In an attempt to articulate this broader point of view I asked Sister Bernadette what she thought about it and made a case for a more Cosmic Communion.

"Couldn't the miraculous journey of store-bought bread be considered its own kind of consecration? How it comes to our hands from a bag in a store, a crop in a field and a seed in the ground by the amazing miracle of Nature and the work of human hands? And what if we were all to eat that bread with real consciousness and reverence? Wouldn't that be a kind of Holy Communion?"

She looked at me as though she understood but then she said, simply, "No, Celia."

> *If God was enough for my happiness, would I*
> *still be searching for answers, for a church, for*
> *a place, for a home, for all the things I wonder*
> *and think about?*

I didn't go back to the Anglican Church. I seemed incapable of walking two paths. In my mind, I had to choose one, and living in a Catholic community made the choice clear: continue to attend the course on Catholicism in London each week and keep an open mind about converting.

The weekly journey to London for the course was like a private field trip, riding the train and strolling through the dark streets of chi-chi Mayfair to the Jesuit Centre, where I would go to evening Mass in the ornate church next door. The walk gave me a chance to follow in Jesus' footsteps because of the queue of hungry people squatting in the rain and asking for money outside the rich shops and hotels. I'd buy food on the way and stop and talk to them, offering them a bar of chocolate or a piece of cake.

The course at the Jesuit centre affirmed what I really love about Catholicism: it understands that whatever God is, it's a Mystery. During the Mass, the priest will say, "The Mystery of Faith," and I always feel that in that moment, he is telling the truth. The course did not, however, address my resistance to the institutionalization of that Mystery. How the power structure of the Institution imposes certainty and righteousness on What Cannot Be Known.

The fall programme at Heaven's House was in full swing and I took part in almost every scheduled retreat, including an Icon Painting course where I learned the ancient technique of the Prosopon School of Iconology by meticulously following the specific stages of drawing and layering paint to create an icon of Saint Michael, the Archangel. It was exacting, frustrating and precise work and I loved it. I wasn't bad at it either!

One of the women on the course happened to mention to me that she was a Lay Carmelite and I expressed my surprise. "I didn't know becoming a Lay Carmelite was even an option!" She told me she'd converted to Catholicism to follow the Way of Carmel and that she had wanted to become a full-fledged Carmelite Sister but was already married and had to settle for the next best thing: being a part of the Carmelite community as a layperson. When I told her about my struggle she asked if there was a priest I could talk to about it.

"Maybe Father Carl," I said, "He's one of the local parish priests and he seems pretty open-minded. His sermons are very forward-thinking, anyway."

"You must go to him and tell him you would like to be received into the Church," she said, frankly. "Until you become a Catholic, all this thinking about Carmel and becoming a Religious is just fantasy." The fantasy word was definitely a red flag. My tendency toward fantasy was no doubt playing into my spinning head, but how much?

The next time I attended Mass at the church where Father Carl was the pastor, I asked him if he would meet with me to talk about my vocation. He said he'd be glad to and we arranged a date and time. I was looking forward to our talk because I admired him. He was intellectual and kind and he had a gorgeous voice, singing parts of the Mass in a silky tenor. The church was a good half-hour walk from Heaven's House and I took my time getting there, stopping to watch the waterfowl feeding in the streams that ran behind the rows of grand houses and praying quietly for the courage to say, "Father, I'd like to be received into the Catholic Church, would you help me?"

Father Carl gave me a cup of tea, and we sat down in the living room of the rectory, surrounded by books and more books. They were everywhere, piled beside us on the floor, covering every surface, lining the shelves that lined the walls. Every once in a while, Father Carl's mother would call out from the bedroom. "She's not well," he told me.

Instead of asking him the direct question I'd rehearsed on the way there, I found myself sharing my reservations and my doubt. Father Carl listened quietly and offered up some of his own experience, telling me a story about a similar confusion he felt while he was in seminary college, training to become a priest.

"The piece of advice I was given was, 'assume you're in the right place for now, until it becomes apparent that you're not.' Or words to that effect." As for becoming a Catholic, Father Carl told me very simply that conversion was "an invitation, not an obligation." This had never occurred to me before. I'd always felt *obligated*. But if I was being called, wasn't I obliged to answer?

"It's a free choice," he said.

"So that means I'm free to either accept the invitation or refuse it?"

"Of course. It will be interesting to see if you begin to long for the Eucharist as you continue discerning. That will tell you something."

The next programme at Heaven's House was an 8-day Centering Prayer retreat. I'd now been practicing this form of meditation for six months and the retreat not only deepened my practice but further introduced me to the humble teachings of Father Thomas Keating, one of the founders of the form. We watched Keating's video series called *The Spiritual Journey* and his friendliness, humour, intellect and openness to psychology and other religious traditions, as well as his love and respect for science, made him a true guru in my eyes.

At the beginning of the retreat, Lynn, the facilitator, offered us all a check-in session and I gave her the short version of my story.

"I'm a convert," she told me in reply. Of course she was.

"How do you get around the doctrine?" I asked her, trusting that I wouldn't be insulting her with the question. Lynn shrugged her shoulders. Ignore it, basically, was her answer.

"Our priest doesn't even say the Creed," she said.

There are various versions of the Creed, the statement of faith that asks individuals to profess their belief in "the Father Almighty, Creator of Heaven and Earth" and "Jesus Christ, his only son … born of the Virgin Mary," who will "come again to judge the living and the dead," and reciting it is normally an integral part of any Sunday service. Lynn seemed to be suggesting that I could become a Catholic and simply ignore the parts I didn't like. While this was an appealing idea, it somehow didn't seem legitimate enough for me. If I were to become a real Catholic, didn't I have to buy it all, hook, line and sinker? What would be the point in converting to a faith only to discard its tenets?

During one of the meals, Sister Martha put on some music. In all the silent retreats I'd done at the Naramata Centre, music had never been played. Retreatants were expected to experience the sometimes uncomfortable silence that arises when people eat together without speaking. Music, it seemed to me, was an escape. Sister Martha asked me, in a whisper, if it was too loud and I nodded, frowning. She went to turn it down and looked at me for confirmation. "More," I mouthed, and continued instructing her to lower the volume until the music was barely audible. When she sat down again I could see she was miffed. But it was quiet! And people were uncomfortable. So they should be, I thought.

The retreat was intense. I'd never sat for so many meditation sessions. There were many moments of deep connection but on the last day, my energy was heavy, and I felt very tired. We had our closing session in the prayer room and after everyone had left, I stayed behind, unable to face coming out of silence to go downstairs for breakfast and socializing and saying good-bye. I knelt on the soft carpet before the icon of Jesus, the Blessed Sacrament to my right, and the wooden carving of the Crucifixion to my left.

"What am I supposed to do?" I whispered as yet more tears pushed up from the heaviness inside of me.

Go out and share this love.

Okay, that's all? I can do that. But what about conversion?

"Take the Plunge," said a book staring out from the pew ahead of me in the chapel one morning, after the retreat. Was it for me? I picked it up. *Take the Plunge: Living Baptism and Confirmation* by Timothy Radcliffe. I searched his name and watched a few of his videos and found him to be a sympathetic radical. So I wrote to him, telling him that I was stuck, for many reasons, but one being that according to the Catechism of the Catholic Church (a collection of Church teaching on various topics), homosexual acts are "intrinsically disordered" and "contrary to natural law" and any orientation other than heterosexuality is "objectively disordered." How was I supposed to get around this?

He wrote back: "Dear Celia McBride, Thank you for your letter. Prayers for you as you discern the way ahead. For me, God is present in every love. This was the position of Cardinal Hume too. The Church is trying to find its way forward on this complex issue. The important thing is that people feel welcomed without reservation. Pope Francis said, on this matter, 'Who am I to judge?' I hope that you do indeed Take the Plunge! May God's grace guide you in all things. God bless. Timothy OP."

Because I had left no stone unturned, another letter arrived, this one from the prioress at the Carmelite Monastery in Notting Hill. I'd written to her from Suvigny after watching the documentary *No Greater Love*. In her letter, she thanked me for writing and invited me to come and discuss my vocation and the possibility of a stay with their community to see if God was calling me to Carmel. I told the Sisters the story of my correspondence, and they somewhat reluctantly encouraged me to go to London to visit the monastery.

Aside from being made famous by the rom-com with Julia Roberts and Hugh Grant, Notting Hill is a lively section of urban London full of antique and second-hand clothing shops and hip foodie destinations. An unlikely place for a Carmelite monastery. One of the most amazing shots in the documentary *No Greater Love* is the last one, where, after 100 minutes of watching the nuns living entirely sequestered in their enclosure, the camera pulls out and up into the sky and the viewer sees that their property is actually sitting in the heart of a major city centre.

When I got to the gates, I rang the bell. Once inside the high, concrete walls, it was as though the noise from the traffic, the bellowing hospital next door, and the scads of people passing by had stopped completely. I had entered another world.

A cobblestone laneway took me to a stone cottage from which a woman and her dog emerged. Together, they escorted me inside the main building and showed me to a waiting room. On the mantelpiece was a photograph of the Little Flower, Thérèse of Lisieux, staring at me with her intense eyes, penetrating me with her famous look, a mix of sadness and knowing far beyond her young years. I smiled at her. She smiled back. "Did you bring me here?" I whispered.

An obese nun in full habit came in and, saying no more than two words, led me to another empty room to wait for the Prioress. I wondered at this Sister's size and what wounds she might be hiding beneath her layers of skin. Why had religious life not healed them? Maybe it had. Who was I to judge?

She pulled back a set of wooden shutters at the far end of the room, revealing an iron gate, which she unlocked and opened. A waist-high wall remained to separate us. The Prioress soon entered and sat on the other side of the wall. She smiled at me. I remembered her dimples and soft Scottish lilt from the film and told her my story easily, as if we were friends. She listened attentively and responded sometimes with a question.

"I have no idea where all of this is heading," I said, "I'm just trusting and following and doing my best to let go."

"Lead Thou me on," she said. I smiled, not understanding. "'Lead kindly Light amidst the encircling gloom, Lead Thou me on.' It's a hymn by Cardinal John Henry Newman." I hadn't heard of him. "He was a convert," she said.

The Prioress said that coming to stay with the community for a month or so would be the first step, but she, like the Lay Carmelite woman I'd befriended on the icon course, reiterated that until I actually became a Catholic, becoming a Carmelite or a Sister of Contemplation or anything else was but a fantasy. When our time was up, she blessed me and thanked me and told me the Sisters would be praying for me. Then she pulled the shutters and turned the lock from the other side.

As I returned to the buzz of the streets, the Carmelite fantasy disappeared with the closing of the heavy iron gate behind me. However much I admired those women and wished I could be that humble and selfless, I didn't have it in me. At least that much was clear.

CRESS

190

N ot long after the Centering Prayer retreat, the Sisters called me back upstairs to their private quarters and invited me to stay for good.

"Really?" I asked.

"We need you, Celia," said Sister Bernadette.

"We LOVE you, Celia," cried Sister Martha.

Part of me was over the moon. It felt so good to be wanted! Another part of me was sceptical. Kit at Mount Carmel had also said, "We need you, Celia." The parallels were a little eerie: two Sisters re-visioning the future of their dwindling congregation discover their saviour in a young leader. The Sisters of Contemplation were determined to continue Father Jacques's legacy. That had been the reason for the Spiritual Internship in the first place. I brought them hope.

"Isn't it all a little quick?" Hennie asked me when I told her, not hiding her own scepticism. Yes, it was, I admitted. Six weeks was not a long time. But there was a sense of excitement between the three of us and the future looked bright. Online, I discovered the option of a two-year visa for religious workers and started to make plans.

Since arriving at Heaven's House, I had been hearing the Sisters refer to Cress, their community on the southern coast, where four more of their Sisters lived, two of them in the convent, once a medieval manor, and two in the adjacent nursing home. The nursing home was owned and operated by the Sisters of Contemplation but was managed locally and employed dozens of local staff. The business operations had become increasingly difficult for their dwindling congregation and Sister

Bernadette had hired a consultant/business manager named Karen to help revamp the nursing home. Sister Bernadette and Sister Martha were also envisioning a different kind of future for the convent/manor house.

"We'd like you to come with us to Cress this weekend," said Sister Bernadette.

"We have an idea of transforming the manor into a spirituality centre," said Sister Martha, "and we're having a meeting with some local friends of the community to discuss the future plans."

Visions of running an interspiritual retreat centre danced in my head but the skepticism needed attending to. On the drive down, I asked the Sisters to say more about what they had meant by "we need you." Sister Bernadette explained that my leadership qualities would be very helpful to them. I had so much to offer their community and they saw my presence as a huge gift. They wanted me to contribute to their vision of how to keep moving forward, how to build and grow Father Jacques' legacy of contemplation. I was glad they didn't just see me as a fixer but rather as a part of the community, someone who had actual skills to offer them, and I let their words of encouragement sink in as we drove the rest of the way in silence.

Soon, the English Channel appeared, shining on the horizon a few short miles away, and we pulled off the motorway onto a winding road, passing a sign welcoming us to one of Britain's "Areas of Outstanding Natural Beauty."

"You see the Downs," Sister Martha said, pointing to the undulating hills that ran alongside us. Sister

Bernadette slowed down as we passed a high, stone wall and she pulled the car through an open gate.

"That's our little church," said Sister Martha, indicating a small stone church to our immediate right.

"And that's the priest's house," said Sister Bernadette, motioning to a little cottage on the left.

"And here's the manor house," said Sister Martha. "The front part is 11th century, as you can tell, but now you can see the addition that was built onto the back in Georgian times." We parked beside a weathered statue of Saint Joseph holding his baby Jesus amidst a carefully groomed terrace of bright tulips, dahlias and cascading greens. I was in awe of my surroundings. The manor looked like something out of *The Merry Wives of Windsor*.

Not twenty feet away from the house was the nursing home, a modern three-story facility now housing forty or so residents, many of whom were dying or in very poor health. Look for the coincidences!

The heavy black door of the manor drew open and we were greeted by two smiling women in habits, Sister Ita and Sister Grace. They were both wearing veils made from the same blue material as their smocks. Sisters Bernadette and Martha no longer wore their veils and this told me something of the Cress Sisters' adherence to their tradition.

"You're very welcome," said Sister Ita, with her country Irish accent. I had met her once at Heaven's House and she seemed glad to see me again. I guessed her to be somewhere in her seventies. Sister Grace, a gregarious Londoner on the cusp of ninety, gripped my hand and shook it heartily. I'd been told she was in the early stages of Alzheimer's and this became apparent during tea and biscuits in the dining room, when she repeatedly asked us all the same questions.

Sister Martha gave me a tour of the manor house, a convoluted maze of empty bedrooms that had once been occupied by Sisters who were now resting in peace in the churchyard next door. She left me alone in the room where I would stay for the night, a small bedroom at the very top of the house with a low, slanted ceiling and a large window overlooking the shallow lake that dominated the three-acre property. It was a cozy, welcoming spot and I named it the Crow's Nest, as it was the highest point in the manor.

From the room's only window, I could see a pair of swans and a family of ducks gliding across the water below. An old yew tree stood directly ahead, its top rising slightly higher than the house, multiple birds flying in and out of its hidden centre. The nursing home, in full view from this vantage point, beckoned.

"I want to live here," I whispered to the yew tree.

Once settled, we prepared to welcome the guests for the discussion regarding the manor's possible transformation into a spirituality centre. Sister Martha had asked me to prepare something, and I'd wrongly assumed she'd wanted me to facilitate the entire discussion. She'd been somewhat offended and had to correct me, but we managed to make the afternoon gathering a success. I gave a little presentation for a handful of the Sisters' friends and supporters using Father Jacques' last name, *Bienvenu*, as a jumping off point and riffed on the translation (welcome). By doing so, I hoped to bolster the vision of a centre where the soul-miserable could be *welcomed* with hospitality and generosity and be given sacred time to retreat from the madness of the world and contemplate peace.

The next day, on the drive back to Heaven's House, Sister Martha said that she had never, in all her years as a Religious, heard anyone connect to Father Jacques' vision the way I had.

"I feel like he brought me to you," I said, repeating the story of the spiritual presence I'd felt in the *poustinia* at Robin Hood's Bay. "I feel very at home at Cress," I added, telling them more about my experience of working in the nursing home in Montreal and how I'd wondered if I'd found my true calling there before being whisked away by the Stratford commission. "Now I end up living in a community that just happens to have a nursing home? I mean, what story is God writing?"

"It is rather a coincidence," said Sister Martha.

In that moment, I did feel like God was writing the story of my life and it did seem incredible. Future fantasies danced in my head. I could live at Cress instead of Heaven's House. I could assist Sisters Ita and Grace in the manor as well as spend time with the remaining Sisters and residents next door in a spiritual-care capacity. Maybe I could even help run the nursing home, and eventually, in good time, form a whole new spiritual community to support the living and the dying of the residents.

When we returned to Heaven's House, I received a phone call from Father Daniel, the Director of the

St. Beuno's Jesuit Centre in Wales. My application had been accepted.

"We're looking forward to having you come for the Spiritual Exercises, Celia, but I'm afraid we will not be able to offer you the Eucharist during your time with us," he said, somewhat sheepishly.

"Oh, that's alright!" I chimed back. "I attend Daily Mass here and receive a blessing instead of Holy Communion so it's fine." He was obviously relieved. It didn't occur to me to challenge him. Yet.

The St. Beuno's retreat would be 36 days long, starting in early January 2015. The six-month tourist visa I was on would expire in mid-February, a week after the retreat ended. The Sisters weren't overly supportive of the idea of my disappearing for the five weeks leading up to my departure, but they were accepting of my discernment process and agreed to let me go. They were clearly buoyed by the fact that I'd begun the application process for the two-year visa, which, if successful, would allow me to return to their community soon after.

It was now December. Sister Bernadette and Sister Martha planned for the three of us to spend Christmas at Cress (Hennie would go home to her family), and I was given permission to head down a couple of weeks early to support Sisters Ita and Grace. On my way, I took a side trip to London to meet up with my sister Melissa. We took in a show in the West End and went to eat dinner in Chinatown. The restaurant was packed with a pre-Christmas crowd, and as we slurped noodles from large bowls of steaming broth, I filled her in on my journey toward conversion and the upcoming retreat at St. Beuno's.

"It's an evil patriarchy," she said of the Catholic Church. Her words were harsh but how could I argue? Melissa had been partnered with a woman for almost a decade. She questioned why I would even consider returning for another two years let alone stay in the community permanently.

"Because there's so much potential," I told her. Even as I said it, I knew my answer followed a toxic pattern I had yet to break: falling in love with potential.

Melissa and I hugged tightly in the madness of Piccadilly Circus and said good-bye. I was relieved to get on the quiet train to Cress after being in the hive of London.

The quiet rhythm at Cress soon proved to suit me as well. It was structured yet unhurried, and the two Sisters moved slowly. Four times a day, we would pray the Daily Office in the chapel, a converted room in the Georgian section of the house. Five times a day, we'd meet in the dining room for breakfast, lunch and supper, plus mid-morning and mid-afternoon tea. Breakfast was self-serve, lunch was a hot meal brought over from the nursing home kitchen, and supper was a light meal prepared by Sister Ita, usually a salad and toast.

Sister Grace did most of the talking, and I responded to her repetition with curiosity, acting as if I'd never heard her stories before. Sister Ita would sit quietly and listen and only occasionally say something. She was often tired because she rarely stopped working. She looked after Sister Grace, doling out her medication and doing her laundry, making her supper and reminding her where she needed to be for prayer and Mass times. She endlessly ironed purificators and albs so that Father William, the resident priest who lived in the little cottage and worked as the chaplain in the nursing home, had everything he needed to say Mass throughout the week. She made sure the church had flowers, picked from the garden by the gardener, and did all the arranging and changing and cleaning of the vases. Her arthritis really bothered her but she just kept on going.

In all of this, I did my best to help. But Sister Ita liked things done a certain way and obedience, it turned out, was not my strong point. I used the wrong tea towel to dry my hands and did the dishes in the wrong order. I asked way too many questions and spoke when I shouldn't have. She would criticize me and I'd go into shame and apologize. Another toxic pattern.

Visiting the two ailing Sisters in the nursing home was a comfort. It reminded me of what I was good at, this form of spiritual accompaniment that required nothing more than being a loving presence and a witness to lives diminished by age and illness. I was good with Sister Grace, too, and sometimes, in the afternoons, we'd walk arm-in-arm to the nearby park, and she would repeat to me the stories of her youth. Sister Grace had once been a "woman of consequence," according to Sister Martha, traveling around France, tracing the steps of Father Jacques, taking pictures and writing essays on the topic. Alzheimer's had made Sister Grace forget what she'd just said but it had not yet deteriorated her wit and intelligence. She was fun to be around.

When I had time alone, I would go for long walks in the surrounding countryside. I loved marching across the grassy Downs. High on the hilltops, the rain and the wind would greet me, and I'd get lost watching the clouds travel across the grey sky. The sea was only a couple of miles away and you could almost taste it in the air.

Christmas approached. The tension between Sister Ita and I fluctuated. Determined to break it, I confided in her my struggle with the church.

"Do you want to become a Religious?" she asked me.

"I think so," I said, "but I'm afraid I'm not cut out for it."

"A rolling stone gathers no moss," she said, "and if you don't try it you will never know for sure."

There was still the small matter of conversion. Father Carl had said that it was "an invitation and not an obligation." He'd also said it would be interesting to see if I began to long for the Eucharist. I wasn't sure if I was longing for it but being *refused* seven days a week was starting to get to me. Three days a week, during the masses at Cress, I would cross my arms before Father William, and four days a week, I'd cross my arms before Father Lorenzo at Moreland, the local parish church. Actually, I was beginning to see the whole business as totally and utterly *unjust*. Would Jesus have denied me his own body? NO! So why was it okay for the Church to deny me Holy Communion? It wasn't.

Evidently, I was not the only one tired of the daily refusal. Father William approached me one morning after Mass and told me it was really upsetting him. A highly-anxious but very kind man, Father William kept his distance most of the time, but we'd started to get to know each other at the midday meal when he would come over to the manor to eat with us.

"But I'm not *allowed* to receive, Father," I told him, when he expressed his dismay at my deliberate arm-crossing every time I went up during Holy Communion.

"Do you need to make a confession?" he asked.

"No, it's not that. I'm not Catholic."

He was shocked. Why wouldn't he be? He'd seen me doing everything right: standing and kneeling and reciting the prayers and remaining silent at all the appropriate times. He'd seen me kneeling alone in deep prayer before and after the Mass, making the sign of the cross on my chest and genuflecting toward the Blessed Sacrament behind the altar, my knee going right down to the ground. He couldn't believe that I was not a member of the Church.

"I'm currently discerning a sacramental baptism," I told him.

"But what are you waiting for?" he asked with exasperation. When I began to share some of my confusion he stopped me short. "You're overthinking it! Do you think Saint Peter went around asking everybody what they thought about it? No! Just get in there!" he said, making sweeping motions with his hands as if he was Saint Peter himself issuing forth thousands of pagans and Jews through some imaginary barricade to the Christian faith.

"It's not that easy," I said.

"Oh, for heaven's sake, just stick your head in the font and be done with it."

His suggestion made me laugh. The idea of sticking my head in the font took away some of the agony of the decision, which continued to weigh on me heavily. "But I've already been baptized!" something inside of me would continue to shout.

> *I feel like I'm losing my mind. I'm trying to convince myself to stay, that this is the place, but what if it's not?*

As the days led up to my departure for the long retreat, I was frantically trying to finish *Last Stop for Miles* with the long-distance help of a producer friend in Whitehorse. In order to make and complete the film, I'd had to keep throwing away my dream of making the perfect movie and continually revise my goal. "It only has to be pretty good," I would tell myself.

"It's pretty good," I finally told my producer friend, as we created the master copy and submitted it to a Yukon festival. We were done.

I could now turn my focus to preparing to depart for the Ignatian retreat. I was feeling really guilty about leaving Cress. The Sisters needed my help, I reasoned, and it was not good for them to be living without some kind of assistance. Leaving them to go on a five-week retreat was selfish. Better to make the sacrifice and stay.

"You strike me as a person who needs to be needed," said Sister Martha, after I offered to remain at the manor.

"They've done just fine without you up until now," said Sister Bernadette, "Stick with your plan."

I decided to check in with my good friend Ellen, one of my supports back in Canada. An astrologer and Tarot card reader, Ellen and I had been exchanging services for four years. I liked the way Tarot cards would speak to my life and, in this particular Skype session, Ellen's reading of one of the cards put forth an evocative question: "What is the lie you are telling yourself?" It was too huge to answer. I decided to take it with me on retreat.

When it finally came time to leave Cress, Sister Ita let me give her a hug and a kiss on the cheek. "I'll be back," I told her.

"But there's no life for you here," she said.

"I disagree!" I said, cheerfully.

"Where are you going?" Sister Grace asked, not for the first time that morning.

"I'm going to Crewe, Sister Grace, to make a retreat."

"O Mister Porter/Whatever am I to do?/I wanted to go to Birmingham/But they put me off at Crewe," she sang, pulling me toward her in a hug. "Come back to us."

RETREAT

MY
CHIEF - SPIRIT

- REFUSES TO BE ANNIHILATED
  BY THE RCC, DOES NOT WANT TO CONVERT
- DOESN'T MIND TOO MUCH GOING
  TO MASS THOUGH GETS IRRITATED OFTEN

MY
VICAR - MIND/CONSCIENCE

BELIEVES IN THE PROTESTANT
REFORMS & SEES BECOMING RC
AS GOING BACKWARD
WOULD LIKE TO BE GOING TO
ST PAULS OR UC OR SOME KIND
OF PROTESTANT WORSHIP
FEELS THAT BECOMING RCC
WOULD ⊏══ BE TO
CONTRIBUTE TO MASSIVE
INJUSTICES   DONE IN
THE NAME OF   LOVE i.e.
PHARISAICAL   LAWS/RULES
THAT EXCLUDE & LIMIT FREEDOM
PPLE

FOURTH ELEMENT
RECONCILIATION
THROUGH
CHRIST

MY - HEAR
LITTLE CONVER[

- ALREADY KNEELIN[
  AT THE FOOT OF THE CE[
  IN THE CHAPEL, HA[
  IN PRAYER, HAPP[
- ALREADY RELEIVI[
  COMMUNION IN HE[
  HEART
- CONTENT TO BE ASS[
- ALREADY RELEIVED[
  THE "CHURCH" i.e. TH[
  MYSTICAL BODY OF CH[

GIVE THANKS TO THE LORD FOR
HE IS GOOD. AND SHE IS EVEN
BETTER.

JESUS HEADED [
THE CITY AND PA[
BETWEEN TWO
FOREIGN STATES. HE ENTERED A

S t. Beuno's in Wales was being renovated, which is the reason I was heading for Crewe, in Cheshire. Sister Grace's song played in my head as the big city sprawl of London turned to working-class towns and wintergreen fields. I stared at the scenery and checked my email, the last time before going offline for nearly five weeks. A newsletter from Diane at the Madonna House in Robin Hood's Bay included a brief note about their summer guests: "Christ himself carries those he chooses to the inn of our hearth and hearts. And what a variety of wayfarers he brings: young people from lands as distant as Korea and the Canadian North West; a woman longing to be baptized and priests of many years needing respite …"

A woman longing to be baptized? Was that me? This perception vastly differed from my own. The phrasing irked and embarrassed me. In my mind, I had been *compelled* by what I thought was a Divine Imperative. I wasn't longing for it. I thought I *had* to do it. And when the visiting priest had appeared that day instead of Father Cian, it had been the Universe's way of saying, "Nope, not today." Why I continued trying after that woeful rejection tells you how ingrained my grandfather Jack's mantra is in my psyche: never, ever, ever give up.

But now I would have thirty-six days to figure it all out, thirty of them in glorious silence. During the Catholicism course I'd taken at the Jesuit centre in London, a woman I'd met there had undergone the Spiritual Exercises of Saint Ignatius the year before. She shared with me what a grace it had been. To have that much time to retreat was nothing less than an "enormous privilege," she'd said. Her words stayed with me as I walked through the streets of Crewe, a once-thriving junction town that now seemed forgotten. The decline of industry had reduced many of Crewe's buildings to a state of neglect and disrepair and I could see the consequences of unemployment and poverty in the people and their homes.

When I reached the retreat centre, called Wistaston Hall, I was relieved to see a big park and open fields just over the road, promising plenty of green space for longer walks, which I knew would be vital to my sanity. I was greeted inside and shown to my room by one of the retreat facilitators. She told me she was a Sister with the Faithful Companions of Jesus (FCJ), one of the more progressive orders I'd discovered in my search for a community the previous year. This Sister wore a pair of pink bellbottoms and a pink-striped t-shirt, immediately winning my favour, and when she told me that two of my fellow retreatants were FCJ novices, I felt a flash of envy.

On the way down to dinner, a book on a stand by the entrance to the dining room caught my eye. It was cracked open to a brightly coloured photograph of cosmic gases colliding in an explosion of reds, purples, blues, blacks and yellows. I read the cover and smiled at the title: *The Hand of God: Thoughts and Images Reflecting the Spirit of the Universe.* My childhood God was saying hello.

Sœur Cécile in Taizé had told me that undergoing the Spiritual Exercises of Saint Ignatius would answer the fundamental question of whether I was being called to religious life and I was determined to get my answer.

The Exercises are essentially a way of determining how God is speaking to your life through consolation and desolation experiences. Time is spent reading through the Gospels, the four books written about Jesus' life, and using the imagination to place yourself within their time, as though witnessing and experiencing their events first-hand. Through prayer, I was to have colloquies or dialogues with Jesus and Mary and God, or anyone else who showed up in my imagination. A daily check-in with a spiritual director would help guide the way.

In my application, I had requested a flexible spiritual director who would allow me to approach scripture from a very broad perspective. I was given Gerry, a Jesuit priest who loved poetry and smoking and had been taking neurotic people like me through the Exercises for a long time. Gerry was so *laissez-faire* that by the fifth day I asked him when we were going to start doing the actual Exercises and he smiled, reassuring me that we *had* started, five days before.

Daily Mass was part of the rhythm of the day and it didn't take me long to figure out that I was the only one not receiving the Eucharist. There were plenty of non-Catholics in our group, they'd made it known during introductions on the first day, but all of them were lining up each evening and receiving Holy Communion as though it were the most natural thing in the world. The sense of injustice at having to cross my arms for a blessing soon turned to righteous indignation. Needing to figure out the exact rules so as to prove to myself (and hopefully everyone else) that all these Protestants were out of line, I turned to *The Catechism of the Catholic Church:*

"#293: When is it possible to give Holy Communion to other Christians? Catholic ministers may licitly give Holy Communion to members of other ecclesial communities only if, in grave necessity, they ask for it of their own will, possess the required dispositions, and give evidence of holding the Catholic faith regarding the sacrament."

"Possess the required dispositions" obviously meant baptism. Okay, so these were baptized Christians, but were they really receiving out of "grave necessity"? And what evidence did they give that they were "holding the Catholic faith regarding the sacrament"? How did the priest know for sure that they truly believed in the transubstantiated Real Presence of Jesus in the bread?

"I'm so angry!" I told Gerry, but he waved it away with a sweep of his hand.

"What a lot of silliness," he said. His light-hearted approach helped, temporarily. Later, I stewed, resenting his ability to be so cavalier about a situation that was now officially torturing me. Seeking further vindication for my anger, I found a quote in the Bible that perfectly justified my wrath:

"In vain do they worship me, teaching as doctrines the commandments of men. You disregard God's commandment but cling to human tradition." ~ Mark 7:7-8

In my view, that rule from the Catechism definitely fell under the dual categories of "the commandments of men" and "human tradition." Yes, refusing me Holy Communion was a lot of silliness but it was also undeniably contrary to the teachings of Jesus, the founder of the faith and the man we were all supposed to be following devotedly.

My contempt for the entire Institution and its pharisaical dogma had brought forth one, crystal-clear thought: ask Gerry to baptize me. As soon as that thought arrived, it was followed immediately by another one: You are ridiculous. I wanted to crucify the Church and join it at the same time. The contradiction made sense. I was being excluded by an unfair rule and an unjust practice. But did I really believe that belonging to the club would take away my pain? Didn't my heart already belong to the Christ-Love? Instead of asking Gerry to baptize me, I prayed for humility, one of the core principles to strive for in the Spiritual Exercises.

A couple of weeks into the retreat, I discovered three distinct parts of myself through the active use of the imagination and deep inner listening. The part of me desiring conversion, who longed to be married to God and wear the habit and serve the Church was, in fact, a very young part of me. This part of me arrived in the form of a little girl, kneeling at the foot of the cross and romantically in love with Jesus, her sweet Lord. She was my heart, and I started calling her the Little Convert. The more intellectual part of me who balked at conversion and was unrelentingly critical of the more exclusive aspects of Catholicism was, ironically, just as rigid as the rules she was rebelling against. This part of me was my intellect, or my head, and I started calling her the Vicar because she was all about reform: the Church needed to evolve and she needed to preach about it! The third part of me, my gut or my spirit, saw beyond the romanticism *and* the rigidity. This part of me knew God through Nature and was more masculine than feminine. He announced himself as Chief. (I realize now this may be culturally inappropriate or disrespectful, and I can only apologize and say that Chief came to me as an authentic, and loving, inner experience. I mean no disrespect to my Indigenous friends.)

No wonder this raging battle had been taking place inside of me! Only one part of me really desired conversion. Yes, it was my heart, and, therefore, some might argue, the part of me that ought to be obeyed, but it was still only one part. My head and my gut were not on board.

It's worth mentioning that I have since learned that these three parts of me could also be called the Child Within (or Inner Child), the Critical Parent and the Loving Parent, and working with all three has become a regular practice. At the time, however, discovering these characters was wholly revelatory and when I told Gerry about them he suggested that something significant had been freed in my interior life. He was right. The walk I took that day had me singing out loud as I tromped through a dewy pasture. During the remainder of the retreat, the pressure of whether to convert lessened significantly and the days of quiet prayer and ceaseless meditation grew richer.

After thirty days, we came out of silence and transferred from Wistaston Hall to St. Beuno's in Wales for three days of review and reflection. I was given a tiny room on the top floor of the castle-like building with an inspiring view of a gleaming, snow-covered Mount

Snowdon and the frosty-green Clywd Valley below. As I contemplated the retreat and all it had taught me, the Tarot card's question suddenly came back to me. "What lie are you telling yourself?"

"I think maybe I've been lying to myself," I told Gerry in our last session.

"What is the lie?"

"That I'm a Catholic nun."

Something went *THUNK* inside of me but Gerry seemed pleased. The Spiritual Exercises had done their job: they had helped me to answer the fundamental question of whether I was being called to religious life. But I felt zero pleasure. That interior *THUNK* just felt plain bad and, therefore, wrong. Perhaps it was that old fear of making a mistake. I didn't know.

Since we were no longer bound to silent meals, spontaneous conversations filled the cavernous dining hall. I opened up to one woman in my cohort about the discernment process I'd been navigating, and she encouraged me to stay in what she called "the liminal space."

"The temptation is to take action," she said, "but if you take action to avoid the uncertainty and confusion, I'd advise against it. Discomfort is not the right reason to make a decision. Stay with the liminality for as long as necessary. It's a gift."

Another retreatant, a young Jesuit novice from the Netherlands, told me his conversion to Catholicism was the greatest joy of his life. "I wake up sometimes," he said, with a dreamy look in his eyes, "and I realize that I have done it, I am a Catholic and I think, 'Yes! This is good. I am happy.'" His smile was like that of a young man in love. "And I want you to know," he continued, "that I respect you so much for crossing your arms each evening during the Mass to receive a blessing. You did what is right. All the non-Catholics who received the Eucharist ..." he shook his head, "that wasn't right."

This young man's remarks brought back the anger over the injustice of this archaic rule, and I decided to talk directly to Father Daniel, the Director. He was in his office and his door was open but he was pressed for time and asked me to come back the next day.

That evening, I was asked if I would participate in the Mass by bringing the bread and wine forward during the offertory chant. This felt like the cruelest joke of all but I did it. During the Eucharistic Prayer, as Father Daniel consecrated the bread and the wine, the thought of being refused Holy Communion yet again squeezed my heart dry like a sponge. But I did it. Father Daniel put his hand on my forehead and looked into my eyes, blessing me with consoling, sympathetic words.

After the Mass, the joyful people filed out, satiated by the glory of the Eucharist and the prospect of sharing a delicious supper together in the dining hall. I stayed in the pew. Total, abject desolation. I could not control my emotions. The figure of Jesus, suffering on the cross, loomed above me. My body shook. "What am I supposed to do?" came my prayer. From within, I heard the words *bear it*.

Bear it. Okay, fine. If Jesus could bear the crucifixion I *suppose* I could bear this. But I still wanted to give Father Daniel a piece of my mind.

The next day he welcomed me into his office and I sat across from him at his desk. He was probably somewhere in his forties and very good-looking. I imagined us going out on a date in another time and place.

"I don't understand why I am being refused Holy Communion when all the others are allowed to receive," I said, bravely.

"Because they've been sacramentally baptized," he said. There it was again: my own baptism was not sacramental and, therefore, could not be recognized by the Church.

"Okay, but the Catechism says non-Catholics should only be given Communion in grave necessity and then only if they give evidence of holding the Catholic faith regarding the sacrament." He looked surprised by the exactitude of my response.

"We try to make the Church's position clear and then we leave it to their conscience. In your case ... it was simply impossible."

"But why doesn't my own conscience count?" He pressed his lips together and looked at me with great sympathy. There was nothing more to say. I shook my head. "I just want the pain to stop," I said.

"The Lord wants your pain to stop, too," he said. I looked up, surprised. He said, "Do you want to be a Catholic, Celia?"

"Say yes!" shouted the Little Convert from somewhere deep inside me. But before I could respond, the resistant Vicar muted the cry. "A part of me does," I replied.

"Well, it sounds to me like you are longing to be united with Christ in the Eucharist."

But I'm already united with Christ, Chief said, quietly. Afraid of Father Daniel's judgment, I could not say the words out loud.

"And if you don't become a Catholic? What is the alternative?" he asked.

"Going on as I have been, I guess. With my own spirituality."

"What about being baptized as an Anglican?"

"I don't see the point."

"Then my advice would be to ask the Sisters you're living with to accompany you in the process of being received into the Catholic Church when you get back."

That evening, in the privacy of my little room, I sat in silence and stared out the window. The grilles were diamond-shaped and centuries-old, and the glass they framed was thin, letting in the February cold and making the radiator beneath the window clink and clunk. The winter sun made the snow shimmer and the Clywd Valley turn golden. I contemplated Father Daniel's questions. Why didn't I see any point in being baptized in the Anglican Church? The different Protestant churches had always embraced and welcomed me. But I was truly fixated on Catholicism. It was the only way to get it right. And hadn't the *THUNK* told me something important? Didn't it mean I wasn't lying to myself about becoming a Catholic nun?

The time had come. I'd just spent five weeks learning the Ignatian way of proceeding, which had taught me to make a decision. Make it, and then spend some time living with it. There will be internal and external experiences that arise from making the decision. Note them. These experiences will either confirm or deny the decision. The option to begin anew will always be available. My mind went back and forth.

"God, just make a decision, Celia!" I said, with a loud groan of impatience. "Okay. Fine. I'm deciding," I said to the valley, calmly and firmly. "I will become a Catholic. Thy will, not mine, be done."

My decision, in perfect opposition to what the Spiritual Exercises had seemed to reveal, brought no response from the valley.

WAFFLING

Back at Heaven's House, I told the Sisters about my decision.

"Oh, now you will be able to receive Holy Communion!" Sister Martha said, clapping her hands together and doing a little jump.

"The Director at St. Beuno's suggested I ask you both to help me with the process." I had a feeling that getting the job done before I left for Canada in a week would be impossible but still, I hoped.

"Of course," said Sister Bernadette. "Perhaps you could speak with Father Eamon about how to proceed." Father Eamon was the Irish Father across the road who would often sit in silence rather than deliver a homily. I liked him. He was down-to-earth and friendly. Maybe he would just stick my head in the font.

"Easter is typically when adults are received into the Church," he said, when I went "over the road" to see him the next day, "and we're only a few weeks away from that now. Is there a way for you to be baptized at Easter while you're back in Canada?"

"I don't know," I said.

"We will support you in whatever way we can," Father Eamon promised. "If you need a reference letter saying you've been coming to Daily Mass for the last six months I'll email it to you. Whatever you need." Clearly, sacramental baptism involved much more than a willing head and a water-filled font.

A few days before my departure, Sister Bernadette invited me up to their lounge to discuss my role in the community upon my return, presuming the visa application would be successful.

"We'd like to try something different when you come back from Canada," she said. "We'd like you to live at Cress and work in the nursing home as a spiritual companion to the residents."

"Really?" I asked, feeling a flood of happiness rush into my system. Sister Bernadette laid out the terms. It would be a paid job, 20 hours a week, for a three-month trial period. I could have my independence, an income and still live and participate in the community.

"You'll be helping Father William with the pastoral care and perhaps accompanying the staff and the families of the residents on a spiritual basis as well. And of course, you'll be a help to Sister Ita and Sister Grace." Sister Martha also brought up the topic of the future of Cress as a spirituality centre and my possible role in that. That was still on the table, too.

"It will be an experiment," Sister Bernadette concluded. Genuinely excited and grateful, I thanked them for the opportunity. It felt just perfect. "And if it doesn't work after three months, well … there isn't really a role for you here at Heaven's House, Celia."

Ouch. That hurt. But my heart had been set on Cress anyway and the excitement had taken hold. I shared the good news with Melissa on a final visit to London the day before my flight. Spring had sprung and this time we walked through Hyde Park, admiring the blooming rose garden and the white cherry blossoms blanketing the trees. She was less than enthusiastic. I knew she disapproved of the path I was choosing but I kept hoping she could be happy for me.

"And I've finally made a decision to be baptized," I said, cautiously.

"You're just looking for attention," she said, rolling her eyes.

"But we're already Catholic!" I responded defensively, "The McBrides were Catholic. If you think about it, the baptism is just a formality." It was a stretch and she knew it.

"Whatever, Celia. I think you're insane and unwell." Melissa had never been one to mince words and these ones cut like a knife. I felt ashamed of my decision and angry at her for judging me, but I also knew her shrewd insight into my character held some truth. She emailed me later that night to apologize but I couldn't deny that her words had further pierced the bubble.

In that last week, Hennie and I had been meeting in her room to do an Examen of Conscience together, a nightly Ignatian practice of reviewing the day. When I'd gotten back from St. Beuno's, I'd asked her to join me as a way of building community and getting to know each other better. We'd been living together for six months but our friendship had always been tentative. Now, as we shared the Examen each evening, we also began to talk more deeply about our individual experience of the Spiritual Internship. We discovered we were both really lonely. The Sisters' vision of them sharing their lives with us wasn't really playing out in reality. Though they had tried to involve us, Hennie and I both felt isolated and alone. Hennie and I really bonded in that last week and when she dropped me at the airport she said, a bit teary-eyed, "See you in two months, mate."

The adventure! The adventure of saying YES
to GOD. To the Unknown.

Instead of heading directly to Toronto for the mandatory in-person visa application, I first flew to Fort Lauderdale, Florida, where my parents spend the winters, and where Jessica and her family were now living. I needed family contact.

As I shared my decision to convert to Catholicism, my father listened with close attention, as he had the previous summer when he'd asked me to explain why I was leaving a good job in Whitehorse to go to England to pursue something he didn't understand. He still didn't get it.

"It's not an intellectual process," I said, "and it's hard to explain with words. It's a call of the heart and I'm trying to find a way to live out that call in a formal way." He asked me hard questions, which I answered as honestly as I could. No, I didn't believe that the Pope was infallible; no, I didn't think a woman's choice to abort a child was the Church's business; no, I didn't think homosexuals were intrinsically disordered; yes, I thought women could be priests.

"So what you're telling me is that when it comes time for you to be baptized and the priest is saying whatever he is saying, you're going to have your fingers crossed behind your back?"

I thought about it. It sure seemed that way. "Yes, I guess so," I said.

"And you're okay with that?"

"I guess I am."

My mother had similar questions and reservations. "What puzzles me is why you can't do all the admirable things you want *without* being part of a religious organization, particularly one as supremely wealthy and powerful, as rife with corruption and greed as the Catholic Church?" I couldn't disagree and had no counter-arguments. When I told her how much I loved the Mass (minus the eucharistic rejection), she agreed.

"I too love the ritual and the liturgy and the hymns. But I just remember when we were in Rome and we saw this parade from the Vatican going by and all I could think was, 'They are *all* old men. Every single one of them was an old, white man.' It disgusted me."

"Would you and Dad come to my baptism?" She paused for a long time.

"I don't know," she said. "Probably not."

Jessica was more understanding. A child psychologist with a scientific and philosophical mind, she'd always had a spiritual side, too, and liked the idea of a Jesus who sided with the underdog. I felt like I could be more explicit with her.

"It's like I need a container, like a way to formally channel my love for the Mystery of God and … I don't have that container. And for all of Catholicism's faults, it also just seems to get it. It gets this desire to be united with that Mystery and it offers me a way."

"Good for you," she said, slathering my divided heart with the healing balm of validation.

Chris, Jessica's biologist husband, wasn't raised with any religion in the home despite being baptized and attending a Catholic school. "We never set foot in a church except to watch someone get buried or married or to humour my grandmother," he told me. As a scientist, he is committed "to explaining the world using measurable, rational processes," but admits to liking agnosticism "because it actually avoids 'rejecting' or 'casting aside' the spiritual." Once, he and I had a conversation about the concept of an "Evolutionary Organizing Principle," which seems to me to be a very good name for God.

One evening during my Florida visit, after a wine-soaked family dinner (water for me), I shared with Chris and Jessica about loving the Catholic faith while fighting the rigid dogma.

"I just keep going back and forth," I told them.

"God is God," Jessica said, with a smile and a shrug.

"Why are you talking about imaginary friends?" asked Chris, in his uniquely sarcastic way.

"God is God," she repeated. Same smile, same shrug.

"If you say that one more time I'm going to divorce you."

"God is God."

Toward the end of my stay, I went to Mass at a Catholic church around the corner from my parents' house. Thérèse of Lisieux, the Little Flower, was front-and-centre, sharing a two-story, stained-glass triptych with Jesus and another saint I couldn't identify. St. Thérèse's colourful panel, lit by the morning sun, did little to quell my slowly-returning desolation. Jessica's support notwithstanding, Melissa's comment about my mental health, my parents' challenging questions, and the staid, white, privileged congregation in the Fort Lauderdale church all contributed to the return of my desolation. So much for making a decision.

> *What if going back to the UK is a huge mistake?*

After an eight-week epic journey that contains enough stories for a whole other book, I headed back to Heaven's House with my two-year visa in hand. The idea of a new life at Cress still excited me and when I was back sitting across from Sisters Bernadette and Martha in their pastel-coloured lounge, watching the tips of the sailboats move back and forth across the distant reservoir, I told them I was really looking forward to the "experiment." I also confessed that my two-month adventure overseas had only affirmed my worldly self and that I'd had a change of heart about conversion. Probably because I did not have the courage to actually say the words, "I've changed my mind" out loud, Sister Bernadette seemed not to have heard me.

"We'd like to invite you to begin an Aspirancy," she said. Okay, she really *didn't* hear me.

"What does that mean?" I asked.

"You aspire to become a Catholic and possibly a novice. We aspire for you to be a part of the community. It would be a time of discernment for all of us. I would accompany you spiritually on my weekly trips down to Cress," she explained. Eight months earlier her words would have been music to my ears. Now I felt my insides shrinking and panic rising.

"How would it be different from what I'm doing now?" I asked, trying to mask my fear. Sister Martha began to describe the deeper commitment that would be asked of me, describing an internal 'cut-off' from family and from the world. "You couldn't just go out and get a boyfriend, for example," she said.

"It would be a time of discernment," Sister Bernadette repeated. No doubt she could see me getting smaller by the moment.

"But we haven't even begun the three-month experiment at Cress," I said, doing my best to sound courageous, "I feel like we need to honour the original plan. Couldn't we revisit this idea after the trial-period of three months comes to an end?"

The moment my words landed, it was as though all the air got sucked out of the room. Both of the Sisters became very polite and then agreed that we should adhere to the previous arrangement. They had only made the offer because they thought it was what I really wanted.

"Let's just see what Providence has in store," I said, again manufacturing confidence to hide the discomfort.

"You're starting to talk like a religious Sister now," said Sister Bernadette, making her own effort to lighten the mood.

Back in the Ivy Room, my mind raced over the conversation. Had I just blown my chance to be a permanent part of this community? To carry on Father Jacques' vision of curing the soul-misery of the world and being the contemplative torch-bearer for future generations? I recognized my grandiose thinking but rejecting the Aspirancy may have snuffed out even a right-sized version of the dream. I was also aware of the sense of freedom I'd experienced when I was back in Canada, on my own, doing my own thing, following my own schedule again. The moment Sister Martha had laid out even the loosest of terms I'd balked.

It was time to head back to Cress. Hennie and I had grown closer before I'd left for Canada, bonding over our shared experience of being isolated spiritual interns, and now she was worried about me. She thought the further isolation and lack of support would be difficult, but I didn't see it that way. At Cress, I would have a purpose.

Before we arrived at the manor, Sister Bernadette took me to the sea. It was only a ten-minute drive from Cress, and we got out of the car to walk along the beach and talk.

"Do you think you're going to be all right living with Sister Ita and Sister Grace?" she asked me.

"I will be if I can come here," I told her. The English Channel was calm and deep blue. The tide was out and the rocky beach was a tapestry of bright and dark green seaweed. The cliffs behind us towered and shone in the midday light. Looking out at the vastness of the water made me feel strong and alive.

It didn't take long for me to slip back into the daily rhythm, and I did my best not to interfere with the symbiotic relationship between Sister Ita and Sister Grace. At the end of the prayer times, I would stay in my chair and wait for the two of them to go out of the room before me, their bodies moving slowly, their hands holding the chairs for support, their veils falling in folds down the backs of their necks like navy-blue tresses in place of their hair, long ago cut short and now hiding beneath the soft material. I would feel so much affection for them in those moments and yet the whole situation was so bizarre that I would also wonder what the f*ck I was doing there.

My imperfections continued to irritate Sister Ita. She would scold me for asking too many questions and overstepping my bounds. There was an empty bedroom just beside me, and I'd helped myself to a duvet and a statue of Mary to improve the Crow's Nest. Sister Ita must have gone into my room while I was in the nursing home because she later made a quiet, backhanded comment about my taking things without asking.

"I'm so sorry," I said to her, "I have always been independent. I'm not used to asking permission. I should have come to you first." She accepted my apology but I was an easy target and the quiet criticisms kept coming. I took them so personally! Once or twice, her comments reduced me to tears. All of a sudden, I was five years old again, lip quivering, giant tears rolling down my cheeks.

Sister Bernadette and Karen, the consultant, were now coming to Cress from Heaven's House for a couple of days a week. During their visits, Sister Bernadette would empathize with my situation.

"Sister Ita has always struggled with communication," she told me, helping me to better understand Sister Ita's character and making it easier to let go of the pain the scolding had caused.

I gained even further clarity into Sister Ita's behaviour when Sister Ita showed me a photograph of all the Sisters who used to live at Cress and I couldn't find her in the picture.

"Where are you?" I asked.

"There," she said, pointing to a slice of darkened shadow behind another Sister.

"Are you hiding?" I asked her.

"Of course," she said. I realized that Sister Ita was not only painfully shy and insecure, but all of those Sisters, her entire community, were dead, lying next door in the church's graveyard. She had been left all alone to care for Sister Grace with little to no support. Her burden was very heavy. Since I could never please her, I decided to stop trying, and the most amazing thing happened. We became friends.

Meanwhile, the battle between Little Convert and Vicar had not abated and I booked a session with Isabelle, a spiritual director I knew back in Canada, who I thought would have a unique perspective on my situation. Isabelle had been a nun, left her order and married a man. Having lived some of her life as a Religious made her a valuable resource.

"So I've got these opposing parts inside of me," I told her, after describing the three characters, "and that's helped me untangle some of the confusion but I must still think that it's God's will for me because I haven't let go absolutely of the idea. I still don't get why God would be calling me to become a Catholic."

"If you understand it before you do it, it would not be a free choice," Isabelle said.

"What do you mean?"

"God's will is to make a free choice," she said again.

"But every time I make a free choice I change my mind!"

"Why don't you hold a council meeting between Little Convert, Vicar and Chief?" she suggested.

That night I spent some time getting quiet and tuning in to these differing parts of me. My journal records the minutes of the meeting:

> *Chief: Don't jump ahead. You don't have to prove anything.*

> *Vicar: Don't do it. You're consumed by scruples.*

> *Little Convert: I want to be baptized.*

> *Vicar: Then I would be saying I believe something I don't.*

> *Little Convert: What don't you believe?*

> *Vicar: Where do I start?*

> *Chief: Okay, meeting adjourned.*

Sister Bernadette had once told me there had to be "an irresistible element to enter religious life" and, at the time, I had thought, "There is!" But what was that irresistible element, really? Was it the notion that living my life as a Religious would somehow render me spiritually perfect? That I would finally be free of all my human flaws? That I would be elevated to a status of such importance that my insecurities and fears would vanish? Yes. But I could not deny that something in me continued to long for Divine Union and religious life offered a full-time devotion to the cause.

> *Dear God, why do you give us monkey minds and then teach us the path to peace is to overcome the mind? Why not just give us a peaceful mind?*

SHIFTING

A DAY AT THE   SEASIDE
ENDS A FIVE-DAY ADVENTURE
LONDON TOWN
EMBRACED ME
AND I
CONSENTED

T he forty-plus residents of the nursing home were men and women from all different backgrounds and different parts of England. This was the final leg of their life journey and I did my best to accompany as many of them as I could, listening to their stories and witnessing their dwindling lives. The work was both exhausting and rewarding. Confronting suffering and death each day was often overwhelming, and I had to navigate feelings of despair and existential hopelessness. Attending multiple cremation ceremonies where entire life stories are told in twenty short minutes begged the question, "What's the point?" and there was never a concrete answer. But there were meaningful moments. Once, a resident with the fever of death brightening and darkening her eyes, gripped my hand and said, "You are here and you are not here." Another, still vibrant but fading, saw angels and described them to me in detail.

Facing suffering and death on a daily basis also generates the kind of gratitude you cannot buy. Similar to the humble appreciation I gained from working at the nursing home in Montreal, I became profoundly thankful for the enormous privilege of the ongoing, moment-to-moment opportunity to *be with* the residents in the last days of their lives. I felt more and more grateful, too, for all the things I would normally just take for granted: I could walk and run and go to the toilet by myself. I could feed, bathe and dress myself. When you can't do these things, life is really hard. What grew inside of me, too, was the affection I felt for all the residents. I began to love them dearly. Just sitting at their bedsides made me happy.

"You must think I'm just a doddery old fool," said Unity, a brilliant painter whose pain would grow worse with each passing visit. The first time I met her she was slumped over her breakfast tray with her face in her toast. We formed a friendship, but her words soon disappeared, and her smile faded. One day, when she could no longer get out of bed, I spent an hour leaning over the bed bars, straining to comfort her. For the next three days I could not move my neck.

Sheila was glamorous and deeply unhappy, full of complaints and criticism of the staff, the food, the nurses. She loved her family and I would ask her questions about them to take her mind off her physical and emotional pain. She remembered "The War" with unbelievable good humour. "We were so happy," she told me, "Oh, yes, we were. Because it brought us together. We had a sense of purpose."

Adrienne suffered with Multiple Sclerosis. With her thinking impaired and her body useless and aching, she'd say things like, "It feels like a poker is jammed up my ass," then open her mouth wide to laugh. No sound would come out but she was in hysterics. One time, her colostomy bag came away from her skin, spilling forth a brown cascade of putrid feces. "That's my shit!" she said.

"I know, stop trying to touch it!" I said. Again, her mouth opened wide in silent laughter.

And Marion. God, I adored her. She'd lived in Montreal when she was young and we talked about our love for the city. She'd cared for her special-needs brother her entire life and still somehow managed to travel the world. Marion would lie in her bed, bored out of her mind, bearing the agony of her ailments. All she wanted was to be outside in the fresh air and sunshine, and on decent days I'd park her chair in a spot in the garden where she could soak up the rays. "Wonderful," she'd say, eyes closed, her already-brown skin bronzing in the heat.

I knew I had a gift for providing spiritual care for the residents of Cress, but since I'd been led to believe I'd have more of a leadership role in the home, I was eager to participate in the larger decisions that were being made. Karen, the consultant hired by the Sisters to improve Cress, seemed to have a different idea. She told me that I wasn't needed at the team meetings with the heads of staff, and this was a blow. I kept my head down, watching and waiting to see how it would all unfold.

Perhaps sensing that I needed some time away, a friend of the Sisters who'd been part of the "let's-turn-Cress-into-a-spirituality-centre" meeting, took me to a retreat day in nearby Canterbury on a scorching July day. The topic, the Mysticism of the Labyrinth, was interesting to me and being in a group of people outside of the Cress community felt good. At morning coffee, I struck up a conversation with an Anglican priest.

"We're not used to this," he said of the intense heat. He had a thick Scottish accent and huge brown eyes, magnified even bigger by his glasses. He was sweating uncomfortably in his collar but his smile put me immediately at ease. When he asked what I was doing there I gave him the truncated version of my story.

"Here am I, Lord," he said. "Send me."

"Pretty much," I said.

"Do you know that passage from Isaiah? The Lord asks, 'Whom shall I send? Who will go?' and Isaiah responds with that line. Utter and complete willingness." I thanked him for seeing that in me and expressed my doubt that I had the same level of humility as the prophet.

After learning about the history of labyrinths and walking a painted canvas version on the church floor, I went out at the tea break to sit under a tree. The dry grass poked my ankles and the hot summer wind kissed my cheek. A deep feeling of loneliness pressed on me when I realized that one year had passed since I'd left Whitehorse. I'd only been at Cress for two of the three-month trial period and I could feel tears coming as I thought of Lukie, the cat I'd left behind. I missed him, missed my apartment, my friends. "I want to go home," I said out loud, and started to bawl.

I need help.

I called a friend for support. "You're beating the crap out of yourself, Celia."

"I am? How come I'm always the last one to see it?"

"Because that's just how good you are at trying to be perfect."

And I kept on trying. In fact, I decided maybe I hadn't really given Catholicism a fair shot. After all, I had never even gone near the Rite of Christian Initiation of Adults (RCIA), a standard course for adults preparing to become Catholics. I'd stayed away from it altogether, thinking it would be the final nail in the conversion coffin, but maybe I'd been wrong about that. Maybe it would open the door. I asked Father William, Cress's priest, if he thought I should do an RCIA course.

"It's not my way at all," he said. "Why don't you ask Father Lorenzo?"

"Contact Gordon, our Deacon," Father Lorenzo offered, when I asked him the same question.

Deacon Gordon, when I rang him up, told me there were no plans afoot for an autumn RCIA course, but he could possibly gather enough people to get one going. We agreed to meet in Cress Abbey, the sprawling park across the road from the manor. It wasn't an Abbey at all, just a lot of land, the remnant of a mansion, now a café, and a high, stone wall surrounding the property. "A rich man's folly," Sister Martha had called it.

"Shall we sit?" he asked, motioning to a picnic table, and we joined a mix of locals and tourists eating ice cream cones in the sunshine. Gordon looked like a retired businessman, clean-cut and carrying a briefcase. "What brings you joy?" he asked me, after hearing the bulk of my woes. I bristled. Joy has been an elusive stranger, something I've had to intentionally cultivate and court. Gordon's question made me feel like I was about to fail a test.

"Going for walks in the high Downs," I said. "Communing with the cows and the horses. I love animals. And nature. I've been bike-riding down to the sea and throwing myself into the waves on my days off," I continued. "Praying and meditating. Dancing, writing, painting, drawing, just being creative in general. But I'm not doing any of the creative practices right now. I mean, I'm journaling and sketching a bit but—maybe that's the problem. I don't have enough of a creative outlet."

"Maybe," he said, "but none of those experiences you've just told me about include people."

"That's true," I said, taken aback by his observation. We talked at length about this.

"You can take the RCIA course," he said, finally, "and I will do my best to rustle up a few people so we can make a go of it, but you cannot make a free decision unless you are in joy. Nor will you ever be able to make yourself fit into this community if it is a round hole and you are a square peg."

> *Okay, God. This is my prayer: get me the hell out of here or give me the grace to stay.*

At the beginning of August, Sister Ita left for a three-week vacation to Ireland. Sister Bernadette announced that Sister Grace would also be going on vacation to a long-term care residence for Religious in London. Being alone in the manor did not increase my loneliness. In fact, my whole body relaxed and I realized how much tension I'd been carrying around on a daily basis. For the first few days I was bone tired. Then, my energy shifted. Having the house to myself brought me, wait for it … joy! I wrote a blog post for the first time in four years. Different from journalling and emails, blogging reminded me of who I was.

Oh, yeah! I'm a writer.

While the Sisters were away, the woman who'd taken me to the Labyrinth Day in Canterbury invited me to a Taizé Prayer evening at a place called the Quiet View. "Oh, you'll love it," she said, "It's in a yurt!"

She picked me up on a Friday evening and we were welcomed very warmly by the owners of the Quiet View, Lizzie and John, a couple in their late sixties. Lizzie, I'd been told, was an Anglican minister but she looked more like an artist to me.

The yurt was filled with chairs and people. Candles were burning, brightening the altar, laden with icons and the familiar cross unique to the Taizé community, which looks like an upside-down bird in flight. A harpist was setting up and I found a kneeling stool and took a place on the floor, closing my eyes and soaking in the peace and warmth of the place.

After the singing-prayer and silent meditation, cake was served. And tea, of course. I was seated next to a woman named Kate, a lady who struck me as very grand and yet very humble. She was in her eighties and she spoke the Queen's English, that fine accent belying good education and privilege, with a deep, low voice. She was eating the cake, a dense, sticky, lemon thing that looked like heaven on a plate.

"That looks delicious," I said.

"It is," she said, with delight. "I'm quite chuffed because I'm the one who made it."

As we continued talking, Kate shared a little bit about her experience hosting the man who had been the special guest of the evening, an African Anglican priest, who had told us the story of losing his home to the war in his country and how he had fled with his wife and children to a refugee camp. He was now in the UK for an ecumenical conference, and he had been staying with Kate.

"The Sisters I'm living with right now have a community in Africa," I told her, as a way of making conversation.

"Oh? Where?" Kate asked.

"I can't remember the name of the country. It's one of the smaller ones with an obscure name." It was Benin but I could not for the life of me think of it.

"Burkina Faso?"

"Close. Something like that."

"Cote d'Ivoire? Birundi? Cameroon? Djibouti?" I was amazed. Kate went on to name a few more.

"How do you know so much about Africa?"

"I've been there many times with the IEF." My next question was obvious.

"It's the International Ecumenical Fellowship," said Kate.

"And what is their primary purpose?"

"The unity of all Christian people," she said. "We want to heal the deep divisions caused by denominational splits."

"Sounds right up my alley," I said.

"We have our International Conference in Prague in a couple of weeks," she said, with a twinkle in her eye.

When it came time to leave, something prompted me to ask Lizzie, our host, if she was a spiritual director. Her kindness and open-hearted energy, her knowing eyes, her powerful singing voice, and her closing prayer, which had addressed God as "She," made me want to talk to her.

"I do accompany people," she told me, "Not formally, but yes, it is something I offer."

A few days later, I returned to the yurt. Lizzie pulled up in a golf cart and we sat in the grass on their hilltop, the afternoon sun warming our backs. A sloping field of hay waved in the distance as I shared my ongoing saga.

"I'm aware of how hard I've been trying to do God's will," I said. "That much I do know."

"I see," said Lizzie, understanding. "What does God's will mean to you, Celia?"

I sighed. The perpetual riddle. "I once heard someone say that God's will is for me to be happy. That's it. So simple. But I don't know if happiness is the point. Doesn't religious life ask that we die to ourselves? Surrender all attachment to happiness? One Sister told me that the moment she'd entered religious life the lights went out." Lizzie shook her head slowly, concern showing visibly on her face. By her look, I knew I was back in perfectionistic territory. "I'm striving to make this work but … it just isn't working."

"Maybe you need to stop striving," she said. I nodded, her words touching the wound.

"I don't even believe in this version of God I've been trying so hard to please."

"She believes in you," said Lizzie. She came around behind me and wrapped me in a red healing blanket, rubbing my back and holding me close.

"This is the God who loves me," I cried. "The One who brought me here to you."

"God's will for us has to be liberation. Because God calls us to be ourselves."

When the tears dried and lightness displaced sorrow, Lizzie said, "I spent a fascinating time on your website and would love to have you bring one of your programmes like *Being Enough* to the Quiet View."

I was stunned. I'd known Lizzie for how long? She'd had one look at my website and immediately recognized what I had to offer. How many months had I been living with the Sisters and not once had they ever asked for my retreat leadership? They'd been so excited to welcome me, all my gifts, all my talents, and, yes, they'd given me a special position at Cress, but never had they said, "Celia, we would just love for you to lead a retreat at Heaven's House."

"If I'm still here, I'd love it, too."

Back to "should I stay or should I go." Having difficulty making a concrete decision. I keep waiting and seeing, letting things unfold. This may be the right thing or it may be fear of choosing wrong.

As I began to let go of striving to fit into the community, the desire to go back to Canada got stronger. But how could I abandon the community and Father Jacques' vision? How could I walk out on the staff and the residents of the nursing home? How could I jump ship three months into a two-year visa? It seemed unthinkable. But spontaneously going to Prague for the IEF's international conference didn't. I decided to ask Sister Bernadette for permission to go despite some trepidation.

"It's up to yourself," she said, a bit tersely, when I rang her.

"The trip lands right around the end of my three-month trial period," I reminded her. "We could meet and have our re-assessment when I get back." She seemed to soften at the mention of the trial period and added how pleased they were with the presence I was providing at Cress, both in the nursing home and in the manor. Sister Bernadette then added that the future of a spirituality centre at Cress was still a possibility.

PRAGUE

P rague was having a heatwave and the hot, dry air felt so good on my skin. I rode the tram to the Masarykova Kolej, where the IEF conference was being held. Through the dirty windows of the old streetcar, I took in the red clay rooftops, the deep green urban forests and the hardy people walking the cobblestone streets of the city. I've been to Paris and Moscow, and Prague is their lovechild.

When I arrived at the Kolej, Kate was waiting for me. "You made it," she said, in her deep, elegant voice. She introduced me to Elias, an eccentric American ex-pat in his seventies who wore a big wooden cross around his neck and a black, gauzy shirt with long flowing sleeves. He had a New York accent tinged with British inflections.

"Two weeks ago we met, providentially," Kate told him, "and here she is."

Elias and I became fast friends. He was an artist and a free-spirit and had been a Catholic monk. He'd fallen in love and left the order but later become an Anglican priest. Now, he'd returned to his Catholic roots. I told him I didn't belong to any church but had been struggling with whether to become a Catholic.

"There really is no comparison. You won't find what you're looking for anywhere but the Catholic Church."

"Will you baptize me?"

"I'd be honoured," he said.

But I knew I'd still be denied Holy Communion. In order for the Eucharist to pass my lips "in the right way" I would still have to be officially received into the Catholic Church through a confirmation process.

Having Elias baptize me would make things *less* illegal, meaning that I could then technically do what the sacramentally-baptized-but-not-Catholic folks at St. Beuno's had done, but it would still not be right by the standards of the Catholic Church.

The conference was a lively event. I was impressed by the truly international membership: a mix of Spanish, French, Polish, British, German and Czech people of varying denominations. Their Christian faith was second nature to who they were. They didn't have to spend hours dissecting it, like I did. These members of the International Ecumenical Fellowship were committed to Christianity as a unified religion, one in which differences were respected and celebrated. We weren't supposed to ask each other "what denomination are you?" because it wasn't supposed to matter. But everyone did ask because it did matter, despite the best efforts of all to make it not matter.

Each day we heard liturgies from each of the different denominations and sang hymns that emphasized "many paths, one Light." The panels were always inclusive, educational, and designed to bring us together. Yet despite the determined commitment to Christian unity, I was struck by how deeply the divisions remained, especially when it came to the Eucharist. The Anglicans and the Lutherans and the other Protestant denominations welcomed all baptized Christians in attendance to "receive," while the Catholic and the Orthodox churches made no such invitation, nor did they partake in receiving from any of the Protestant denominations. This made for some tense moments.

"Whatever about transubstantiation," an Anglican priest said to me in an unguarded moment. "It's insulting for them to refuse our offering."

"The Sacraments are what distinguish the Roman Catholic Church," Father Luke, a Roman Catholic priest, said to me during a breakfast chat on the subject. "This is where we truly meet God. And you cannot receive these gifts unless you give yourself first to the Church that administers them, which in turn gives you Christ in the Sacraments, and all the grace that is given by each one is then yours, fully and … *this* is why," he said, buttering his roll with an easy shrug.

Knowing that my baptism of desire didn't count for anything sat like a dead weight inside me. During a Liturgy of Creation service, I made my way to the altar and crossed my arms before the female minister whose long, black hair tumbled down over her white robe and stole. She was covered in tattoos and looked like a biker.

"The Body of Christ," she said, holding out the bread. When I did not uncross my arms she frowned disapprovingly, lifted the bread higher and fixed my gaze.

"It's the Body of Christ," she said, her words tinged with impatience. I took the bread in my mouth and felt the tears come.

"Well, that was really quite embarrassing," Father Luke said to me as we all made our way outside, back into the late-afternoon heat.

"What happened?" I asked.

"The minister … she insisted I take the bread. I went up for a blessing just to be a part of the ritual, out of respect for everyone else but she practically forced me to take it. It was really very awkward."

How could two people have such wildly differing responses to the same gesture? For me it had been an act of mercy, however forcefully executed, but for Father Luke, being urged to accept bread consecrated by a non-Catholic had been an embarrassment. In that moment, I felt so sure that Jesus would never have approved of this sacramental dividing line, the cause of centuries of such unbearable conflict (and still going on to this day), that I had no desire to belong to any denomination.

"But choosing and belonging to a church community is what it means to be Christian," said Angela, a German woman with whom I'd bonded quickly that night at dinner. "You will never find a church that suits you one hundred percent. I work with a lot of Jews and even they struggle with how to belong to their faith. So you do the best you can with the church you do belong to."

On a free afternoon, I discovered a bustling town square alive with tourists and locals eating in outdoor restaurants, performers juggling and building human pyramids and hucksters selling their wares. Delicious smells drifted from a jumble of local and international food stalls at the edges of the square, where working horses stood patiently waiting for their carriages to fill with riders.

In the square's centre, dominating all of this activity, was a gigantic sculpture of a larger-than-life man leading a crowd of people to freedom. It was Jan Hus, the hero of the Czech people. The IEF conference was honouring the 600th anniversary of Hus' execution and I'd learned that Hus had opposed certain doctrines of the Catholic Church. He had been branded a heretic and burned at the stake. His enormous figure now hovered over the chaotic square with a silent, commanding power. Six-hundred years later, many were still fighting for the Church to officially reinstate his name. "The Church takes 500 years to make a change," Father William of Cress had once said to me. But if Hus' name still hadn't been cleared 600 years later, what chance did any present-day inclusive reform really have?

The last day of the conference, Sunday, was reserved for the Catholic liturgy. We were bussed to the Brevnov Monastery just outside of the city to attend a Mass celebrated by the resident Benedictine monks. The sun was already burning hot at 9:30 a.m. and I found a bench in the shade to sketch the church dome and its shadow.

Just before ten, the bells called us to Mass and we filed in, following the monks and the ministers and priests from IEF, all wearing their robes and stoles, all heading to the altar to say the Mass together. Mammoth stone columns and colourful frescoes depicting scenes from the life of Jesus decorated the cavernous space. This was a special ecumenical occasion and we had been told that all were welcome to receive Holy Communion that morning. No doubt this invitation had been made with the assumption that everyone at the conference was a sacramentally baptized Christian. What to do?

After the priests consecrated the bread and wine, they asked us to form a circle around the entire perimeter of the church. We must have been at least 200 people, and now we stood beside one another in a giant ring of unity while the monks went around, offering the Eucharist to each person.

I was one of the last ones in the circle and this gave me plenty of time to panic. If I received Holy Communion would I be deceiving and disrespecting these monks? Was I just being overly scrupulous? I no longer knew what was right and what was wrong. As the priests drew closer, I became more and more distressed.

A woman got down on her knees and the priest placed the Body of Christ on her tongue. She was only two people away from me. "What to do, Lord? What to do?" The priests were beside me now. I turned to look behind me and there was Elias. Our eyes met and he smiled.

"I don't know what to do," I whispered. He saw my distress, and I saw my whole predicament run through his mind in an instant. Without hesitation, he beamed love and said, "Receive."

The monks were before me. I knelt down on the stone floor as I had seen the woman do.

"Tĕlo Kristovo."

I opened my mouth. He placed the "flesh of God" on my tongue.

"Amen," I said, bowing my head, making the sign of the cross.

Beauty. Love. Christ.

PART FOUR
RISING UP

DECIDING

TO COMPANIONING
THE ELDERLY IS WHERE
THE ENERGY IS RIGHT
NOW. MEETING THE
NEED.

Septermber arrived, and there was no mention of the three-month trial period at Cress coming to an end. The Sisters didn't bring it up, probably because they found it easier not to, and I just kept waiting to see what would happen. Life went on.

In the first week of that month, Sue, my friend from Madonna House, came to England to visit me. She had actually left the MH community a number of years earlier, but her 15 years with them still informed her thinking, and she'd been an invaluable long-distance support for me as I navigated my common life with the Sisters.

When I'd first arrived at Cress, I'd asked Sister Bernadette if I could have friends come and stay with me. Her response had been firm. "It's a convent, Celia." But after a while, when she saw that I was lonely and suffering from a lack of contact with people my own age, she reversed her decision.

Hennie and I picked Sue up at Gatwick airport. Sue would stay at Heaven's House for a couple of nights and come back to Cress with me for one night. Sister Bernadette and Sister Martha happened to be away on their summer vacation and so Hennie, Sue and I would be alone together at Heaven's House. Miraculously, in that short time, the three of us found what Hennie and I had been seeking for so long: community. Hennie and I both remarked on the fact that we had not felt this particular kind of togetherness while living with the Sisters.

I had texted Sister Bernadette to see if I could borrow the car to drive Sue to Cress to meet the Sisters and to see the manor and the nursing home. Not hearing back, but certain Sister Bernadette wouldn't mind, Sue and I took the car anyway, and she was welcomed with open arms at the manor by Sister Ita and Sister Grace.

Sue, being Catholic and accustomed to religious/community life, fit right in. But then she made herself a grilled cheese sandwich and burned the bread, filling the house with smoke and setting off the fire alarm. Sister Ita was gracious about it, but being in charge of the kitchen for most of her life, couldn't entirely hide her irritation.

I showed Sue the grounds and introduced her to the staff and some of the residents. She, too, had worked with the elderly and was a natural. We both began to fantasize about her coming to live at Cress. She could join the community and expand the vision of the spirituality centre with me! But I was a square peg in a round hole, and Sue knew it.

"What are you doing here, Celia? Are you out of your fucking mind?"

"I know," I said. "I know."

The next morning, when it was time to go, Sue said to Sister Ita, "Thanks for letting me burn your house down," and Sister Ita burst out laughing.

"Maybe you'll come back," Sister Ita said.

"Maybe I will," Sue responded.

At the airport, Sue said, "Listen, I don't know if you're supposed to become a Catholic or not but if you do, it's like a credit card with unlimited spending. It's like the Gold Card. But if you don't become a Catholic you still get the credit card. You still get the like, $5000 or whatever."

Sue had never told me it was better to be Catholic and I don't think she was saying that now. She was talking specifically about what becoming Catholic would mean for my journey. My sense is that she knew I felt the sacrament of Holy Communion to be a Divine gift and if I converted to Catholicism there would be no limit to its value in my life.

When I dropped the car off at Heaven's House, I was confronted by a text from Sister Bernadette. She was not impressed that I hadn't waited for her answer before taking the car to Cress. I apologized, again proving that obedience was neither a virtue I possessed nor had managed to acquire.

> *Went to my first RCIA session. Thoughts of complete rebellion. This will never happen. And the child, the child who just wants to be married to Christ? A sacrifice.*

Not long after my return to Cress, Sister Ita invited me to accompany her and Sister Grace to an annual meeting of the Brothers and Sisters of the Diocese. The "Day for Religious" took place at a 13th Century Carmelite monastery, and the speaker was Sister Margaret O'Shea, a woman probably in her eighties, slim and neatly dressed in a grey suit and cream-coloured blouse, and with the energy of someone half her age. She spoke eloquently and honestly, with wry humour.

"Put the mission ahead of yourself," she said to the room full of nuns (and me). "We must have honest sharing with one another and a little bit of *fun*! Community is having a united spirit and religious life is meant to give us life. Jesus came to bring us life. You can't say, 'I don't want this calling.' You either receive it or you don't. Yes, God will find you where God wants you to be, but more importantly, you have to have a group where you can be *free*."

Everything she said filled me with excitement. What am I waiting for? I wondered. When we returned to Cress I asked Sister Ita what she had thought of Sister Margaret. "She was very down-to-earth," she replied.

"Maybe we could have a community meeting to work through some of our challenges," I suggested. Sister Ita gave me a look.

"That's not your place," she said.

Okay, not so free. I sent an email to Hennie and Sisters Bernadette and Martha, offering Sister Margaret's points about community life as a possible way forward for the four of us. Only Hennie replied with a "hear, hear." When the Sisters came down to Cress on their next visit, they said nothing about my message.

"Do you think we could have a community meeting?" I asked Sister Bernadette. Since my arrival a year before, I'd been the only one to request and advocate for community meetings. Yes, Hennie wanted "community," but she found the forced communication of the meetings uncomfortable. The Sisters were always obliging, but it was clear they also found the meetings mildly intolerable. Nobody *really* wanted them but me. Nevertheless, a date was set and we arranged for my return to Heaven's House the following weekend.

Just before I was about to leave, Sister Grace broke her leg in the darkness of the early morning before breakfast. I heard a thump-thump-thump on the stairs, and then, "Oh bother!" The light was dim but I could see Sister Grace sitting on the bottom step. I helped her up and she hobbled over to a chair. We took her to the hospital and X-rays determined a fracture in her fibula. She was given a boot and a room next door in the nursing home. Secretly, I knew this incident was a huge relief for Sister Ita because Sister Grace really did need more care than she could provide. I wondered if it was a nudge for me to make a move, too.

Divine Intervention.

Back at Heaven's House we had our community meeting. I took a risk and said that the overall situation wasn't working. As hard as we were all trying there was just no real sense of community happening in either house.

"Sister Margaret O'Shea said during her talk that it's very difficult to make a community of Religious and laypeople work," I told them. Hennie remained quiet. The Sisters did not disagree.

"It's true that you and Hennie will never be able to understand us," said Sister Martha. "I'm sorry but you just can't."

Sister Bernadette seemed relieved that I'd named the elephant in the room. The pressure was off. It's not working, she agreed, and admitted that perhaps the two of them didn't even want to live with a lay community. They liked their privacy and were set in their ways. But they appreciated us and they needed us. Maybe we'd have more success if we stopped trying to "be a community" and just let ourselves be what we were: a sort of fractured group of people working for a common purpose. A new freedom seemed to come out of that meeting simply because we'd all acknowledged the truth of the situation, and I felt hopeful that things would work out.

That night, Hennie watched *Last Stop for Miles*. She came to my door when she'd finished, and before I could say anything she burst into tears. I guessed that her emotional reaction was coming from the film's heavy themes of trauma, alcoholism and grief, but when she asked "What are you doing here?" in a pleading voice, I realized she was referring to something much deeper. Now that she'd seen a true representation of my artistic self, Hennie could better understand my square-peg-in-a-round-hole status with the Sisters and the Church. Her tearful plea contained an element of not wanting to see me shrivel up and die here.

Hope for the common life had been generated from the community meeting, but Hennie's tears had affirmed my creative, worldly self. This meant the inner tug-of-war accompanied me back to Cress, where a meeting with Karen, the managing consultant, hung over my head. The three-month trial had turned into five months and counting, and Karen had continued to mention the need to "discuss my role." We'd finally made an appointment to meet in private.

Karen and I had a complicated relationship because we shared meals and the intimacies of community in the manor, but her managerial position made her my boss, which I resented. I considered Sister Bernadette to be my true boss but she was unable to attend the meeting. I also resented that Karen had not wanted me at the team meetings and her fixation on my credentials triggered my insecurities. What she didn't seem to get was that the Sisters had given me the job because of my gifts, not my CV points. There was definitely a competitive tension between us. I'd once told her my profile on the Myer-Briggs Type Indicator (a personality test) was ENFJ (amounting, briefly, to "leader of the people"), and she had completely negated it, saying she'd studied the profiles for years, and I'd probably answered the questions in a way that skewed the results.

I'd also had to report an incident in the nursing home to Karen, and it had not turned out well. One of the residents, Joan, had told me, in tears, that the carers ignored her when she needed to go to the toilet. Karen took my report seriously at first, but when the carers told her they took Joan to the toilet regularly and blamed Joan's dementia, Karen came back to me and suggested I take more training to learn about Alzheimer's disease.

"I don't care if she has dementia!" I wanted to shout. "If somebody thinks they need to go to the toilet you take them!" But she was the boss, so I said nothing.

For our private session, I met Karen in the office she and I were supposed to be sharing. In order to stay out of her way, I didn't use it. It was too stressful. Now, I felt anxious being alone with her.

Karen stuck to her script about defining my role in the home and encouraging me to improve my credentials. I felt myself becoming emotional. A lump formed in my throat. It was humiliating to be crying in front of this woman who had questioned my competence. This would only validate her perception that I was not a leader. I explained my tears by confessing that my time with the Sisters had been really painful and confusing. Karen suddenly softened and told me she understood. She'd been working with religious communities for ten years, she said, and she knew it wasn't easy. She affirmed the work I was doing and suggested again that we look into further training credentials to enhance my role in the home. I left her office and tried to apply the Ignatian principle of humility to what had just happened: be independent of the opinions of others; become willing to be misunderstood; if shown a lack of appreciation, accept it without bitterness.

Back in the quiet of the Crow's Nest, I hit my knees and buried my face in my hands. My breath slowed, my thoughts got quiet. "Lord, what the hell do you want me to do?" I whispered, then waited.

> *Not this. This is not a requirement. You have misunderstood. If you delight in it, yes. But it is not a requirement.*

"What is my calling?"

> *The only place I am calling you is to the cave*
> *of your heart. Where I dwell. To be with me.*
> *In the cave of your heart.*

Call it Conscience, call it Lord, call it the Still Small Voice, call it Intuition. Whatever you want to call It, It speaks.

This communication was followed by an email from Melissa with a link to an article titled, "Pope's fine words on homosexuality are useless while the Catholic Church still calls it a sin." She wrote, "Perhaps you see yourself as some sort of reformer who will incite change from the inside but I think joining something with the intention to change it is egomaniacal. How can you actually join an organization whose core values are opposed to your own?"

That evening, I confided in Sister Ita the contents of Melissa's message. "But you're not gay," she said lovingly, convincingly. I didn't have the heart to tell her that it wasn't just about my sister, that I was a bisexual person and my beloved queer friends were not "intrinsically disordered." Even if I had been as straight as Sister Ita believed, there was just no getting around the staggering injustice of the Catholic Church's ongoing refusal to welcome *all people* to the proverbial table.

I called Sue for support. "First of all, you don't have to be in the convent to live your vocation, and second of all, I think you need to start planning your exit strategy."

"But what about the two-year visa!" I exclaimed. "How can I leave the Sisters after all they've done for me, after all we've envisioned for the future? I can't possibly leave Sister Ita now. The betrayal would be monumental. It's unforgivable."

"Is it?" Sue asked.

"Look, I know it's not working and I'm pretty sure I've decided not to convert but leaving *feels* unforgivable."

Sue told me the story of wanting to leave her last job: she'd known she needed to quit but was terrified to make such a big change. She'd been going back and forth over the decision for months until one morning, when she'd arrived at work, her office chair was gone.

"The *one chair* that I used everyday, that was mine, was gone. Just gone. And when I asked my co-worker where my chair was, she goes, 'Oh, it got sent back to the warehouse.' So be on the lookout for the metaphorical chair getting sent back to the warehouse! That's when you'll know it's time to go."

After we hung up, I stared out the window at the yew tree swaying gently in the wind. A flock of little birds chattered noisily as they flew in and out of its branches. That yew tree had been a comfort to me all these months and I often talked to it like an old friend.

"What do you say, Tree? Should I stay or should I go now?"

The next day, after breakfast, I came back upstairs to the Crow's Nest to get ready to go next door to the nursing home. I looked out the window and froze. The yew tree was gone. I looked down at the garden. A crew of men in hard hats was standing around the massive, severed trunk. Huge blocks of the tree were lying in chopped pieces all around it. It looked like an Ent crime scene. The feathery dark green branches were being fed into a large machine and chewed up by menacing metal teeth. I called Sue and left her a message, "I think my chair just got sent back to the warehouse."

We were now in December and Sister Bernadette asked me if I was going back to Canada for Christmas.

"No," I said, surprised by her question. "I hadn't planned on it."

"Well, none of us are going to be around so if you don't want to be alone perhaps it would be best for you to spend time with your own family?"

"Well," I said, building myself up to tell her the truth, "I'd be afraid that if I left I wouldn't come back."

Sister Bernadette eyed me carefully. "Don't leave us just yet," she said. "Sister Ita needs you here." Then she added her standard response: "Stay on the path, Celia."

On my way over to the nursing home that morning, I met Father William. He'd decided to retire and was nearing the end of his time at Cress. It was a cold, misty day, and the damp clung to everything, moistening our faces and curling the fallen leaves on the soggy grass.

"How goes the search?" he asked.

"I don't think I can take the plunge, Father," I said, stopping short of telling him I was thinking about leaving altogether.

"Well, you're an unofficial member of the Catholic Church, anyway," he said, patting my shoulder.

"I can live with that."

"Keep searching," he said with a wave of his hand as he toddled on ahead.

But the search felt like it was finally over. God was not calling me to become a Catholic. God was calling me to be myself.

When it came time to book my ticket, a one-way flight seemed out of the question. The thought of actually abandoning the Sisters still felt like too much to bear. So I booked a return ticket. I'd go back for three weeks to spend Christmas with my sister Clara and her family, who now lived in Toronto, and have some down time in my parents' empty house in Port Hope.

The day before my departure, Sister Martha, Sister Bernadette, Karen and Hennie came down to Cress for a Christmas lunch. Hennie would drive me and Sister Martha back to Heaven's House that evening, and I would fly out the next day. The five of us spent half the day sitting in a five-star restaurant acting as if everything was okay. Sister Ita looked miserable. She was heading out the next morning as well, and we both had a lot more packing to do.

When we got back to the manor, I told the Sisters I still had a few things to do and went up to the Crow's Nest to finish packing, which took me longer than I thought it would. Then I went over to the nursing home to say good-bye in case I really wasn't coming back. At Marion's bedside, I told her how much I admired her and enjoyed our friendship. "You're talking like this is the end," she said.

"Well, I could die in a plane crash," I told her. She waved her hand to dismiss the idea. After saying good-bye to as many of the residents as I could, my heart breaking, I met Karen at the front door.

"There you are," she said. "Sister Martha is anxious to leave."

I felt a rock in the pit of my stomach. Had I kept them waiting?

"You take the front seat, Sister Martha," I said, as we were getting into the car.

"No," she said, and got into the back. When Sister Bernadette came out to see us off, she said to Sister Martha, "Why are you sitting back there?" as if to imply that I had assumed my place in the front. The tension was unbearable, but I didn't know why. I waved to Sister Ita from the car, wondering if I would see her again. We drove in silence until I turned to ask Hennie how she was doing. The headlights behind us reflecting in the rearview mirror shone a strip of light on her eyes, and I saw that she was weeping, quietly. "This is why I am leaving," I thought.

When we arrived at Heaven's House, I was hoping the three of us could talk it out. I wanted to share with Sister Martha that I had a desire to leave for good, to hear why she had been so quiet and reserved on the drive, and to give Hennie the opportunity to communicate her pain. But Hennie disappeared into her room and Sister Martha announced that she was going to bed.

"You don't want to have a meal together?" I asked.

"No, no. Have a good trip," she said, turning away from me and and going up to her apartment. I knocked on Hennie's door and she let me in. What was going on?

"She was angry that you made us all wait for you," she told me. I felt terrible.

"But why didn't she say anything?" We both knew the answer. Communication was not the Sisters' strong point. Hennie's unwavering loyalty to them meant that she would stay in a situation that made her cry, but that didn't mean she expected the same thing of me. She had become my biggest ally.

"If you come back here, I'll murder you," she said.

LEAVING

Being back in Canada felt a bit like being given a get-out-of-jail-free card. After two days I'd decided to stay. I emailed Sister Bernadette and asked if she and Sister Martha would be available for a Skype call, and we set up a time to connect. I was nervous but resolute. Looking at both of their smiling faces on the screen told me they had no idea of what I was about to say, which surprised me. Sister Bernadette's suggestion that I leave for Christmas had led me to believe they were, at least on some level, wanting me to go.

"I first want to apologize for the last evening at Cress," I said, "I had no idea I was making you all wait, I should have told you how long I was going to be and I'm so sorry I didn't communicate with you better." Sister Martha appreciated the apology but she dismissed it as no big deal. Now came the hard part. "I've decided not to come back," I told them. They were shocked. I was shocked that they were shocked. I honestly thought they were going to say, "We've been expecting this." But they had no idea.

"I blame myself," said Sister Martha.

"Please don't," I said. "This is where my heart is, that's all." It felt like the best way to explain the situation. It was simple and true and it avoided any drawn out discussion.

"We respect your decision and we want you to be happy," said Sister Bernadette. "We want you to do what's best for you and we certainly don't wish to force you to do anything, but perhaps you would like to think about coming back and leaving properly."

My spirits sank. Her use of the word "proper" expressed my worst fear: that I was essentially "doing a runner," an English expression for leaving a restaurant before paying the check. But I worried that if I went back to leave properly I'd guilt myself into staying. Not knowing how to respond, I told the Sisters I'd pray about it and let them know.

I did pray about it. And I obsessed about it. And I consulted practically everyone I came into contact with. All this fresh turmoil made it very tempting to avoid going back altogether. Avoid the conflict, avoid the *difficult*. Just leave the nuns and stay in Canada and forget the whole entire thing. I was under no obligation to go back! Why should I?

God's will is to make a free choice. Liberation.

Then something happened that decided it for me. I got a text from Melissa saying, "Do you expect me to make the eight-hour trip to Cress and back to fetch my bicycle?" That cocksure question was the deciding factor. Melissa had loaned me her bike months ago and I had a responsibility to return it to her. I contemplated paying to get it shipped or asking Hennie to take care of it for me. But no. This minor duty to return Melissa's bike made clear my major duty to return to England and the Sisters of Contemplation. I had to leave their community in a dignified way. Avoidance was not an option.

Next came the tougher question: how long should I go back for? One or two weeks didn't really fit the definition of leaving properly, but four weeks seemed way too long and would likely reignite the desire to stay to please others. I decided to go back for three weeks.

> *Last night in Toronto. Fear and regret are threatening to overtake me. Feel also like a schmuck for leaving Sisters sooner than I was supposed to.*

Once I was back in the UK, I knew I'd done the right thing by returning. There was enough time and space to say goodbye to everyone. But the decision to leave for good felt right, too. At least it did for the first little while. Then the voices of self-recrimination got very loud: "You are deserting the residents, disappointing the staff who became your friends. You are turning your back on Sister Ita, who allowed herself to get close to you." More fresh turmoil.

"You have to do what is right for you," said Sheila, the resident who had told me that wartime was the happiest time of her life. She didn't want me to leave. She said it would break her heart, but she encouraged me because even she could see it was right. "Do what is right for you," she repeated. "For a change."

This is where Christianity can really mess with your mind. Following Jesus means laying down your life for others. Being Christ-like means *sacrificing yourself.* These commands make it so very difficult to "do what is right for you" because they imply that putting self-care and personal well-being first amounts to nothing less than outright selfishness. Clearly, you don't have to be a Catholic to have Catholic guilt!

My doubt increased when Sister Ita, who had been supportive at first, began to treat me the way she had in the beginning of our relationship: punishing me with silence and passive-aggression. If I stayed I could make her happy. Nevermind betraying my own conscience.

"But have you made the choice in good conscience?" Sister Grace asked me after I shared with her how sad I felt, how hard it would be, how upset Sister Ita was. (Despite having Alzheimer's, Sister Grace could still proffer wisdom.)

"I think that I have," I said.

"Well, then, bon voyage!" she said, happily, "and may we meet again in heaven."

An email arrived from Sister Bernadette inviting me to come back to Heaven's House to have some time to talk as a community and reflect on the "deeper reason" for my leaving. When I asked Hennie if she knew why I'd been sent the email, she confessed that she had demanded to know of the Sisters why they were letting me go so easily. She had wanted them to see what they were losing in me. Surprised, the Sisters had insisted that they were simply honouring my choice. While I appreciated Hennie's support, and was secretly glad her charge had made the Sisters question their understanding of the situation, Sister Bernadette's invitation for more communication would force me to tell them the truth. I was taking off because I was truly unhappy in the community, precisely the difficult conversation I had wanted to avoid.

Back at Heaven's House, the four of us sat in silence in the Sisters' upstairs lounge. Grey light poured in. No sailboats in this January cold. Only bare branches and penetrating rain. Sister Bernadette asked me if I'd be willing to share more about my reasons for going. It couldn't be avoided. I looked at Hennie. She was looking at the ground.

"Because I don't really have a voice in this community and if I'm going to live in community I need to have a voice. I need to have a say in how we live together, and how decisions are made, and I need open, honest communication. And I know we've all been trying to do that with these meetings, and I know we even took the pressure off having to make it work but … it's still not working. For me. I understand that the community model I would like to live in is not your model and that's okay. But I can't live with this model."

Sister Bernadette's response was swift. "You're right," she said, immediately. "We've been living by a medieval model. It really is time to change. So … let's try it. Let's create a new model."

It was my turn to be shocked. I kept expecting them to let me go with a huge sense of relief. Not because they didn't like me but because I made their lives more difficult by making demands they simply couldn't meet. But instead of admitting they couldn't meet them they just kept on trying to adapt. "It's okay!" I wanted to say, "You don't have to keep trying to change! Be yourselves and I will be myself and we'll just say good-bye already!" But Sister Bernadette was not one to give up easily, even when it was the smart thing to do, and apparently neither was I.

"Sister Martha and I will come to Cress for the weekend. We'll take time to have a retreat and pray. It will be a time of community and we can discuss how to move forward in a new way."

Someone needed to run the House, so Hennie would not be coming, which was practical but ridiculous. How could we discuss a new model of community without one-fifth of the community?

"You'll figure it out," Hennie said, before I left. My stomach was in knots.

Back at Cress, Sister Ita could not hide her delight. "I've been praying for you to stay," she confessed, on our way to morning Mass at Moreland.

"Maybe your prayers have been answered," I told her, still wanting to please. Maybe I *could* stay on for a few months to see if the new model had legs.

After the Mass, Father Lorenzo, who'd been told about my decision to leave by Sister Ita, took me aside and offered to baptize me. "You've been coming here faithfully for all this time. You've proven yourself to me and to all of us. We could do it in 15 seconds with one witness and no strings attached," he said.

"What does 'no strings attached' mean?" I asked.

"No obligation to the Church."

Here was what I'd been waiting for. An offer to stick my head in the font. Sister Ita was heading toward the exit, people were milling around. It didn't seem like Father Lorenzo meant right at that very moment. We would be coming back the next day.

"Thank you, Father," I said, "I'll pray about it."

When I called Sue that evening to tell her, she said, "If a priest offered to baptize me with no strings attached I'd take it."

Sister Bernadette and Sister Martha arrived that afternoon just as Karen was heading back to London. "Have a good retreat," she said to all of us. Over the course of the week, neither of us had said anything to one another about my leaving and we said nothing about it now as she headed out the door.

The four of us sat together in a circle that felt more like a line, with the three of them on one side and me alone on the other. There was a brief discussion on the purpose of our retreat: to consider how to create a new community model. Having nothing to lose at this point, I took a breath and said that if the Sisters wanted to allow me to have a voice in the community, they would have to hear things they were not going to like.

"We're open to that," said Sister Bernadette.

My sharing began with the unrest at the nursing home and how many of the staff had come to me with complaints and dissatisfaction in the way things were being run. Sister Bernadette immediately got defensive, but I didn't stop there, voicing my concern about their desire to turn Cress into a spirituality centre when they were struggling to manage Heaven's House. This time, it was Sister Martha's turn to get defensive. Sister Ita started to speak but then stopped herself and remained silent.

"Alright, we're getting a bit defensive, I'm sorry," said Sister Bernadette. She said she'd heard me and would look into some of the issues I'd brought up. We closed with a prayer and parted for the afternoon, which had been set aside for silence and meditation. I used the time to journal:

> *What is right for me? To leave. Why are you thinking about staying? For them. How did I put myself in this position of having to make these decisions? CONTROL. Having these kinds of major decisions to make must be a way of staying in control. If I have no decision to make I simply have to accept my life as it is. Commit to BEING.*

It struck me then that my desire to have a voice in the community was really about me wanting to tell the Sisters everything I thought they were doing wrong. They were making decisions without me but of course they were! It was their Order, not mine. I wanted to be in control and I wasn't. I was fighting against my powerlessness but to what end? A square peg cannot fit in a round hole.

The next morning, the four of us went to Moreland for Mass. I hadn't told the Sisters about Father Lorenzo's offer of a 15-second baptism. I imagined myself saying "yes" and all the old arguments returned. I imagined myself saying "no" and the Little Convert grieved. I knew one thing for sure: I didn't want to *make it happen*. I wanted to see if it would or wouldn't happen by a natural flow, an evolving course of events. If I simply let things unfold one moment at a time, which Way would open?

When the Mass was over, I approached Father Lorenzo as he was taking off his vestments. Just as I reached him and started to speak, Sister Bernadette came up alongside us and asked if she and Sister Martha could have a word with him.

"We'll just be a minute, Celia," she said to me.

"Celia could stay," said Father Lorenzo.

"No, if you could just wait outside. We won't be long." said Sister Bernadette.

I went outside the church to wait. It was raining softly. I smiled to myself as the wind blew through the trees and whipped the rain sideways. I had let things unfold: I had approached the priest to discuss the baptism, Sister Bernadette had approached to speak with him about an unrelated issue, I was asked to wait outside. Yes, I could have intervened. I could have said something or *made* something happen. But I took the unfolding as spiritual guidance. I had been shown the Way: it wasn't to be.

That afternoon, the four of us met again in the lounge. Sister Ita pulled back the heavy, red velvet drapes that kept out the cold and the damp. Beyond the centuries-old latticed windows, Saint Joseph held his baby Jesus in the bare winter garden. A strip of blue sky and moving clouds could be seen above the trees. The chairs were still in the haphazard circle that left me facing the three of them. I dug my feet into the thick, red shag carpet while Sister Bernadette said a prayer.

"We are all invited to share now," she said, "about ways that we can help the community move forward, bring it into the 21st century." She and Sister Martha looked at me, expectantly. Sister Ita was looking at her feet.

"Thank you for the opportunity to retreat and to pray," I said, "I was journaling last night and … I realized something about how powerless I feel here. And vulnerable. And that kind of vulnerability inevitably sets up my desire for control. And so I realized that the voice I really want to contribute is actually a controlling voice. It's the voice that wants everybody else to change."

Taking out my journal, I read to them what I had written the day before: "I don't think I'm being asked to stay and pursue a life here …" My throat tightened, and the corners of my mouth pulled down as I fought hard not to cry. "I can choose to stay and God will approve. I can choose to go back and God will approve. Whatever God is, It is only calling me to Wholeness. If I choose to leave, God will find me where I am. And even if I am making a huge mistake, God will write straight with my crooked lines. The world is my home. It does not always satisfy me and yet I am a woman of the world."

After a pause, Sister Bernadette spoke. "That was very moving," she said, with tears in her eyes. Sister Martha was looking at me with tenderness, and Sister Ita looked deeply stricken. I so wanted to know what she felt, what she thought, but I knew she couldn't, wouldn't tell me. Ever.

"Why are you crying?" Sister Bernadette asked me.

"Because it hurts to leave."

"Then why are you going?"

"To be free."

"I never kept you from doing anything you wanted to do," Sister Ita said, quietly, gravely.

"I know that." She was right. I hadn't been imprisoned by the Sisters or the community or the convent or the Church. I'd been imprisoned by my desire to please a God who did not require pleasing.

"Well," said Sister Martha, "If your vocation is freedom, then it's best that you go and live that way, isn't it?"

Later, when Sister Bernadette and I were alone, she said, "I'd like you to think about coming back to start a lay community at Cress. It's what Father Jacques wanted."

"It is a beautiful vision," I said.

At Sunday Mass the next morning, when I went up for a blessing, Father Stephen, who had replaced Father William and knew well of my journey, made the sign of the cross on my forehead and said, "In the name of the Father, the Son and the Holy Spirit, Celia, may you be brought to the waters of baptism by the Lord … in due time."

As I walked back to my seat, I heard the inner voice speak:

> *I have already been brought to those holy waters. I have already been baptized. And I am already a monk.*

POSTSCRIPT

When I left Cress, I landed back in Port Hope, needing time to sort myself out. Six years later, I am still here. The Yukon is my spiritual home, and though I miss the mountains and the bush, I also like this little heritage town and its proximity to rolling corn fields and the majesty of Lake Ontario. Living in my parents' home has afforded me a kind of worldly/contemplative hybrid existence. My father says that the three of us have a "symbiotic relationship," meaning our sharing of their house is mutually beneficial. I am of service to them in myriad ways and they charge me cheap rent and let me use the car. I still wrestle with the angels of privilege and poverty. Gratitude and humility break up the fight.

Those first few months after leaving the Sisters were about working through the grief of both the loss of the community and the death of my fantasy. Living my life as a Catholic Religious was a beautiful vision, as beautiful as the vision of Cress becoming a spirituality centre, but it was an idealized dream and, though it came from the ineffable love of God that makes me who I am, it was still a dream. Letting go has only been made easier by the fact that I made such an earnest effort to make the dream come true. I *tried*. Lord knows I tried. Didn't I tell you I was a perfectionist-addict? This is why I remain committed to carrying out all my spiritual practices on a daily basis. My crazy mind necessitates it.

I continue to learn and grow. Whenever I think I have it all figured out, Life throws me a curve ball and says, "Not yet."

A friend who read a later draft of this book asked me what part the childhood sexual trauma played in motivating the journey to the convent. I'd never actually thought about it. It literally did not occur to me. She, on the other hand, saw the trauma all tangled up in my desire to become a Catholic nun, and bravely marked the connective tissue for me: always doing, achieving, running; running toward safety and running to self-punish; never stopping because stopping is not safe.

> *I will get caught and hurt. Run to safety. Run*
> *to certainty.*

My friend was able to see the connection between the trauma of being pushed out of my little body and split off from my wholeness, and my adult desire for the "wholeness" of Holy Communion. Somehow, maybe, I had seen being given permission to receive the Eucharist as a way "back in," and a way to become whole once more. Her insight was enlightening and validated a quiet truth: these kinds of wounds unconsciously (and seemingly unendingly) drive our actions. As I said, the healing work of making the unconscious conscious is ongoing. Overcoming shame seems to be a lifelong friggin' process. The creation of this book has helped me to shine even more light on the shadows and I'm grateful for that.

As for church, I went back to St. John's in Port Hope, where I'd sung in the choir in the early 2000s, but lost all patience when the Anglican Synod voted down homosexual marriage in July 2019, and I stopped going not long after. These days, I'm seeing a man and learning how to be together while tending to my monastic heart. He and I spend weekends together, and Sunday mornings have become the Church of Relationship. That might be my next book.

I still love the Catholic Mass and still go, on occasion. I go to churches where I am not known because it gives me the feeling of being anonymous, which I like. It is as close as I can get to the intimate, private experience that I cherished in all of those daily masses with the Sisters. Nowadays, when it comes time to receive the Eucharist, I mostly do the right thing and cross my arms. Other times, I rebel and receive. I think Jesus, a rebel himself, prefers it when I take him in my mouth.

Whenever people ask me why I decided not to become a Catholic or a nun or a monk or whatever you want to call it, my stock answer is this: *because everything I was searching for I already am.* I thought I had to *become* something but I Already Am Everything. We All Are.

Since there is no longer anything to become, I find myself in an ongoing process of un-becoming. It's not always pretty, hence the pun. Spiritually, I continue to be a work-in-progress. When people ask me to identify my spiritual beliefs, I usually say "salad-bar" or "interspiritual," my new favourite label. I am a yogi, wannabe Buddhist, follower of Jesus, lover of Christ. "Christ is the Energy that frees us," a friend said. God, yes!

When I talk about my vocation, I describe it only as "touching lives," and I'm given opportunities every day to live it. Providentially, I ended up with a job in a nursing home providing spiritual care for residents, staff and families. It is definitely the gift that keeps on giving. When confronted with the inevitable suffering and injustices that arise from the complex arena that is long-term care, I allow myself to rage at God, the Great Mystery of Existence: "Do you really think this human experiment is working? You might be the Cosmic Spirit of Unity Behind Everything but things are really f*cking messed up down here!" Sometimes there is nothing to be done but allow God to love me in my desolation.

I also have a satisfying and successful spiritual direction practice. My clients range from trans youth to atheist elders. I even have a client who is a Roman Catholic priest. His mission has always been to put people first, and he has had his knuckles rapped by his Bishops countless times for baptizing babies, marrying couples, and performing funerals for the people whom the Catholic Church deems unworthy of the sacraments.

Recently, when I told this renegade Father a bit of my story, he was so distressed to hear that the "unbaptized" barrier continues to keep me from legally receiving the Eucharist that he offered to baptize me immediately.

You know what? I just might do it.

ACKNOWLEDGMENTS

My parents have given me everything.

I started to write on my mum's typewriter when I was eight or nine years old. She was writing a novel, I was writing a novel. Mine was the length of a short story but you get the idea. She is the reason I'm a writer.

Jamie Cowan and Sabina Harpe, friends with editorial skills and creative minds and spiritual hearts, edited the first draft of *O My God*. Without their generous feedback, I could not have written the second draft. Jamie asked the right questions and Sabina knew what needed cutting.

Polly Moore, a friend who writes beautifully and reads voraciously, edited the second draft. "It's missing a narrative through-line," she told me. Her insight and notes were indispensable.

I asked my friend Laurie Davis to edit the third draft. In addition to her editorial skills, I needed her wit, her humour and her cynicism. "It sounds like you're trying to run for Prime Minister," she said. Time to get real in draft four!

Andrea Skinner, a woman who literally speaks poetry, gave the fourth draft a generous edit, providing much-needed praise and encouragement and helping me see where I could go deeper still. The fifth draft got her final approval. Her support was like having a whole squad of cheerleaders in the room with me (but a lot less crowded).

Proof-readers Janet Munro and Wren Brian gave their keen eyes to later drafts. Their grammar and punctuation skills were invaluable. A number of friends along the way read the book and offered critical feedback and morale-boosting (and found more typos—if you found a typo, bravo!). All of these fine people deserve my thanks for helping me to place the book in your hands now.

In the last couple of years, while I was re-writing, the COVID-19 pandemic rocked the planet. It is strangely missing from these pages. Maybe that's a good thing. To remember the world before it happened.

Many of the names and places have been changed. Many of the people I met and the connections I made and the experiences I lived have not been included. God knows I would have liked to tell you *everything*. But a little Mystery is perhaps a good thing, too.

REFERENCES

*Jesus: Uncovering the Life, Teachings and Relevance of a
Religious Revolutionary* by Marcus Borg

Centered on Christ: A Guide to Monastic Profession by
Augustine Roberts, OCSO

Canticle of Daniel 3:57-88, 56

What is Contemplation? by Thomas Merton

Quote from "Catechism of the Catholic Church":
https://projects.flocknote.com/note/544805

Mark 7:7 English Standard Version Anglicised

Mark 7:8 New American Bible

Lizzie and John Hopthrow, The Quiet View,
www.quietview.co.uk

All drawings and journal entries by Celia McBride

ABOUT THE AUTHOR

C elia McBride had a career as a theatre artist and filmmaker before becoming a spiritual director and retreat facilitator. *O My God* is her first book. To read more about Celia or to contact her, please visit celiamcbride.com